CRITICAL STUDIES OF
KEY TEXTS

George Eliot's

Middlemarch

D1362493

Other titles available in the series

Nicola Bradbury
Charles Dickens' Great Expectations

Suzanne Raitt
Virginia Woolf's To the Lighthouse

CRITICAL STUDIES OF
KEYTEXTS

George Eliot's
Middlemarch

T. R. Wright

University of Newcastle upon Tyne

HARVESTER
WHEATSHEAF

New York   London   Toronto   Sydney   Tokyo   Singapore

First published 1991 by
Harvester Wheatsheaf
66 Wood Lane End, Hemel Hempstead
Hertfordshire HP2 4RG

A division of
Simon & Schuster International Group

Typeset in 10½/12pt Sabon by
Keyboard Services, Luton, Beds

Printed and bound in Great Britain by
Billing and Sons Ltd, Worcester

British Library Cataloguing in Publication Data

Wright, T. R.
  Middlemarch.
  1. Fiction in English. Eliot, George, 1819–1880
  I. Title II. Eliot, George, *1819–1880*. Middlemarch
  823.8

  ISBN 0–7450–0618–3

---

1 2 3 4 5   95 94 93 92 91

Contents

Note on the Texts

All references to *Middlemarch* are to the 1988 World's Classics edition, edited by David Carroll for Oxford University Press. The text of this edition is identical with that of the 1986 Clarendon Edition, also edited by David Carroll for Oxford University Press, which has a detailed critical apparatus, recording manuscript and proof variants as well as published textual differences. All quotations are followed by references in parentheses first to the chapter (in Roman numerals) and then to the page number on which they occur.

Other page references in brackets after quotations are to other works by George Eliot and George Lewes abbreviated as follows:

Clarendon: Clarendon Edition of *Middlemarch*, edited by David Carroll (Oxford: Oxford University Press, 1986).

Essays: *Essays of George Eliot*, edited by Thomas Pinney (London: Routledge & Kegan Paul, 1963).

Letters: *George Eliot Letters*, edited by G. S. Haight, 9 volumes (New Haven and London: Yale University Press, 1954 and 1978).

Life: *Life of George Eliot*, edited by J. W. Cross, 3 volumes (Edinburgh: William Blackwood & Sons, 1885).

Notebooks: *George Eliot's 'Middlemarch' Notebooks*, edited by John C. Pratt and Victor A. Neufeldt (Berkeley: University of California Press, 1979).

Problems: *Problems of Life and Mind* by George Lewes (last two volumes edited by George Eliot), 5 volumes (London: Trübner, 1874–9).

Acknowledgements

My academic debts, as will soon become apparent, are many and various but I would like to thank a number of George Eliot scholars by name for their teaching, their help and their example: William Baker, Dorothy Bednarowska, Gillian Beer, David Carroll, George Levine, David Lodge, Graham Martin, William Myers, K. M. Newton and Sally Shuttleworth.

I would also like to thank the University of Newcastle upon Tyne for granting me sabbatical leave during the summer of 1989, when much of my work was done, and the librarians of the Robinson Library, especially Dr Lesley Gordon, for their patient assistance. My deepest gratitude, as ever, is reserved for my wife, Gabriele, who helped me considerably at every stage of the work.

Preface

'Fred's studies are not very deep,' says Rosamond Vincy of her brother, 'he is only reading a novel' (xi, 83). She had obviously not read *Middlemarch*, perhaps the most difficult and demanding of all the loose baggy monsters produced in the mid-Victorian period. Trollope doubted whether any young person could read it with pleasure while Virginia Woolf called it 'one of the few English novels written for grown-up people'.[1] Not only its length, but also the sheer density of its complex web of meanings makes *Middlemarch* a book which requires, and improves upon, re-reading. Hermeneutic difficulty is part of the experience of reading *Middlemarch*, which is a novel about interpretation, exploring the ways in which we 'read' each other and the world. It is a sustained reflection upon 'the meaning of life', an epic treatment of the constantly disappointed attempt to make sense of the world.

Each individual reading of *Middlemarch*, even by the same person, produces new areas of interest, bringing the concerns of the time of reading to bear upon those of the time of writing, just as *Middlemarch* itself is a reflection of the early 1870s upon the early 1830s. All interpretation involves a dialogue of this kind, as the section of this book on the critical reception of the text will illustrate. My own concerns are post-modern, particularly alert to the 'ache of modernism' of which Hardy wrote in relation to *Tess of the d'Urbervilles*,[2] that questioning of previous certainties about God, the self and the world which comprises the most significant historical and cultural context of this novel. 'Nothing is fixed,' complained a contemporary of Eliot's in 1871, lamenting the way in which 'the elements of the old order' were dissolving before his eyes.[3] *Middlemarch*, I want to argue, records that process of disintegration at the same time as attempting to halt it.

If, as Lyotard suggests, modernity is characterised by an appeal to a 'metadiscourse' or 'grand narrative' that places all other forms of language or knowledge,[4] *Middlemarch* is clearly 'modern'. It displays a lingering nostalgia for the 'lost narrative' of Christianity, which it attempts to replace with liberal humanist alternatives (what Lyotard calls the myth of the liberation of humanity and that of the speculative unity of knowledge). Lydgate can be seen to embody two of the principles which characterise modern attitudes to knowledge, 'that of deriving everything from an original principle' and 'that of relating everything to an ideal'.[5] *Middlemarch* honestly records his difficulties while continuing to applaud his ideals. It reveals what has been called 'a double consciousness', aware both of the need to continue the search for 'truth' and of its inevitable failure, holding out a vision of human fellowship while revealing 'the conflicts that obscure and complicate' such a vision.[6] It therefore requires a double reading, alert both to its characteristically 'modern' project and to the ways in which it anticipates the post-modern abandonment of that aim. The grand narratives of the nineteenth century (of which none are grander than *Middlemarch*) contain within themselves, as Lyotard recognised, the seeds of their own disintegration.[7]

The reading of *Middlemarch* which I offer in these pages, informed by the perspectives outlined in the section entitled 'Theoretical Perspectives' can be labelled post-modern in the sense that I abandon all attempts to impose unity on the novel, focusing instead on the play of voices in the text, which represent a multiplicity of language-games whose truth-claims can only be relative. *Middlemarch*, as I will attempt to demonstrate in 'The Play of Voices', is not a straightforwardly mono-logical text, imposing a single meaning upon a transparent reality, but a dialogue between a variety of voices conducted with a keen awareness of the opacity of language, its embed-dedness in particular ideologically-determined modes of per-ception. There is a controlling narrator, or rather a narrator attempting to impose some form of unity upon the text, but even this voice is tinged with uncertainty, as well as being sexually ambiguous.

To read *Middlemarch*, then, is not to be provided with a number of solutions to the problems of modernity but to be provoked into exploring profound questions about the construction of the self (Chapter 2), the meaning of history (Chapter 3) and the death of God, or more literally, the role of religion in the absence of an authenticating metaphysical centre to the universe (Chapter 4). It is also to be confronted with the restricted role of women in a patriarchal society (Chapter 5) and the whole process of change – if and how 'reform' can be achieved (Chapter 6). It is difficult to resist the post-modernist tendency to place this and other significant words in inverted commas in recognition of their problematic status, a tendency anticipated by George Eliot throughout this novel.

The Prelude to *Middlemarch* itself raises all these questions. Its opening words about 'the history of man' and the way this 'mysterious mixture behaves' initiate a complex dialogue with the reader about 'reality' (here not only a problematic term but a quotation), the demands of idealism, the search for a satis-factory 'object' of 'faith', for 'knowledge', for 'scientific certi-tude' about 'the nature of women' and about the kind of society which would not leave their longing for 'unattained goodness ... dispersed among hindrances, instead of centering in some long-recognisable deed' (Prelude, 3–4). These ques-tions are not answered definitively: there have been vociferous critical debates on whether *Middlemarch* is positive or nega-tive about human potential, whether it is fundamentally tragic or comic, whether it portrays a desperate decentred world or a 'mature' acceptance of human limitation, whether Eliot sym-pathises with the aspirations of her ardent heroine or detaches herself ironically from them.

The very title of the novel is radically undecidable. Are we to read a celebration of middle-class progress, a triumphal march of personal and political reform, or a meditation upon failure, the reduction to middling mediocrity of its aspiring heroes and heroines, 'moving with kindred natures in the same embroiled medium' (xxx, 238)? The word 'provincial' in the subtitle is similarly ambiguous, open not only to a straightforwardly descriptive but to a pejorative reading as a reflection of the inability of Middlemarch to accept the innovations of its more cultured and cosmopolitan characters. A march, of course, is a borderland, 'a tract of debatable land',[8] and this, for me, suggests that the most productive way of approaching *Middlemarch* is to see it as a medium for the reader's reflection upon the big questions of truth and meaning which it raises. There can be no single unified 'true' reading of the novel, only a tracing and retracing of the different strands of meaning to be found in its pages.

I

Contexts

Historical and Cultural Context

Among the many quotations cited in George Eliot's notebooks for *Middlemarch* are the well-known lines from Matthew Arnold's 'Stanzas from the Grande Chartreuse' which present his nostalgic persona

> Wandering between two worlds, one dead,
> The other powerless to be born. (Notebooks, 78)

Arnold's mournful meditation upon the position of mid-Victorian intellectuals, brought up in a Christian faith still dear to them but no longer credible, must have appealed to the mature George Eliot, whose own youthful evangelicalism had been similarly undermined by the combined influences of higher criticism of the Bible and scientific rationalism. She steadfastly refused to return to the comforts of supernatural religion, resolving like Marx 'to do without opium and live through all our pain with conscious, clear-eyed endurance' (Letters III, 366). But she remained emotionally tied to the pre-Victorian period of her childhood, whose assumptions were beginning to be challenged in the years in which *Middlemarch* is set (1829–32). 'Her roots', as her husband came to realise, 'were ... in the pre-railroad period' (Life I, 7–8). Intellectually, however, Eliot could not ignore the astonishing changes brought about by scientific and mechanical discovery, changes which made the world of the time in which *Middlemarch* was written (1869–71) an entirely different place to that of the 1830s. The split time of the novel reflects a split within its author, a division between the dead world of her childhood and a future of which she was very uncertain.

A reflection upon the multiple significance of the word 'railways' begins Eliot's meditation upon change in her 1856 review of the first two volumes of Wilhelm von Riehl's *Natural History of German Life* (1851, 1853), a book which celebrates the openness to change of the enlightened bourgeoisie, in contrast with the conservatism of the peasantry and aristocracy. Opposition to change, as Eliot explains, comes in the shape of that philistinism which Arnold was to attack so mercilessly in the 1860s and which is the target of much of the satire in *Middlemarch*. This is how she defines Riehl's philistine:

> the *Philister* is one who is indifferent to all social interests, all public life, as distinguished from private interests; he has no sympathy with political and social events except as they affect his own comfort and prosperity, as they offer him material for amusement or opportunity for gratifying his vanity. He has no social or political creed, but is always of the opinion which is most convenient for the moment. He is always in the majority, and is the main element of unreason and stupidity in the judgement of a 'discerning public'. (Essays, 296–7)

The same sarcasm towards 'public opinion', the same impatience with provincial philistinism, will be found in *Middlemarch* itself. One of Eliot's motives in writing, it has been suggested, was to create a more discerning community of readers who would be open to the changes needed to bring about the brave new world to which Eliot and Arnold aspired.[1]

For liberal humanist reformers, such as Eliot and Arnold, intellectual change preceded political change. One of the most important contexts in which *Middlemarch* should be read, therefore, and one which is perpetually infiltrating the text of the novel to form a classic case of intertextuality (the sharing of a common discourse between different texts), is that of contemporary science, which was bringing about a totally new perception of the world. 'Science', it has been observed, 'was creating a reality not available to common sense'.[2] Its new hypotheses were weaving a web of previously unobserved connections, a labyrinth of explanations which attempted to make sense of a world for which conventional religious beliefs no longer seemed relevant, a world no longer to be seen as a stable, fixed reality but to be described in terms of complex patterns of relationship. In the words of George Lewes's five-volume exploration of *Problems of Life and Mind* (1874–9), the last two volumes of which Eliot saw through the press after Lewes's death in 1878, 'the search for *the thing in itself* is chimerical: the thing being a group of relations' (Problems II, 27).

Science, Lewes argues, resorting to an analogy to become popular with structuralists a century later, has no access to an uninterpreted objective reality: 'Facts are mere letters which have their meaning only in the words they form' (I, 296). Detailed observations only assume significance within a theoretical context or framework. That confidence in 'the presence of undeviating law in the material and moral world', of which Marian Evans had been so certain in the 1850s (Essays, 31), had given way by the 1870s to a recognition of uncertainty about everything: 'What we call laws of Nature are not objective existences, but subjective abstractions' (Problems I, 69). The laws, in other words, originate in the observing consciousness rather than the external object.

The metaphors of web, labyrinth and channel which recur throughout the novel are themselves part of that contemporary scientific discourse which was constructing a new, less certain world. Not only Lewes but Darwin, Mill, Tyndall, Bain and Herschel can be found discussing the 'web' of connections it was the business of science to make.[3] Lewes, drawing upon one of the dominant myths in *Middlemarch*, said that science had placed 'in our hands the Ariadne thread to lead us through the labyrinth' (Problems I, 26) but it was a more fragile, more tangled thread than had previously been thought. Tyndall, lecturing in the 1870s on 'The Unseen Universe', described the world as composed of endless intertwined 'cables of feelings. ... That is all there is.'[4] Such images have particular resonance in a post-modern, post-structuralist age which sees

the role of the critic as a disentangling of such linguistic struc-
tures of feeling, an untying of the different discourses of which
all texts are composed, including those cultural codes which
comprise our understanding of the world.[5]

It was John Tyndall who recognised most explicitly the role
of the imagination in scientific enquiry, seeking in his lectures
of 1870 on *The Use and Limit of Imagination in Science* to go
beyond the chaotic world of appearances and aiming, like
Lydgate, to 'lighten the darkness which surrounds the world of
the senses'.[6] His explanation of optical illusions makes him the
most likely candidate for the role of 'the eminent philosopher
among my friends', responsible for the famous pier-glass
image in *Middlemarch*. That image emphasises the subjective
nature of the vision which imposes a false order, an illusory
grand narrative, upon the random scratches on the glass's
surface (xxvii, 217). Another candidate, however, is Herbert
Spencer, who wrote in *The Study of Sociology* (1873) of
standing by a lakeside in the moonlight and observing the bar
of light created by the moon on the water appearing to follow
him when he moved. Such phenomena, Spencer insisted, had
no 'objective existence' outside the observer. It was a matter of
the framework of perception within which the individual was
working.[7]

Spencer's discussion of the relation between the individual
organism and its social medium employs yet another metaphor
to be found throughout *Middlemarch*, that of a stream cutting
itself 'a large and definite channel' through a resistant material.[8] This metaphor was to prove popular with many
association psychologists, suggesting the manner in which
morality could be seen as a matter of habit, the gradual
construction of a well-trodden path for the emotions to follow,
the establishment of patterns of behaviour which could
become automatic (and could also be passed on to future
generations as acquired characteristics). It can even be said to
have provided a surname for the heroine, whose brook of
altruism is seen at the end of the novel to have infiltrated the
resistant fibres of her society.

Contexts

Echoes of another eminent scientist of the period, Thomas
Huxley, have also been found in the novel. His recognition of
the need for a human moral order superior to the cruel cosmic
order responsible for so much of the suffering in the world was
to find its fullest expression in his work on *Evolution and
Ethics* of 1893. His *Lay Sermons* of 1870, however, drew
attention to the limits of human perception. The 'wonderful
silences of a tropical forest', he argues, are 'due only to the
dulness of our hearing'. If we could actually hear the constant
murmur, 'we should be stunned, as with the roar of a great
city'.[9] Both the suffering and the insensitivity find their way
into the text of *Middlemarch* in the famous passage relating to
Dorothea's first inkling of Casaubon's unspoken sufferings:

> If we had a keen vision and feeling of all ordinary human life, it
> would be like hearing the grass grow and the squirrel's heart
> beat, and we should die of that roar which lies on the other side
> of silence. As it is, the quickest of us walk about well wadded
> with stupidity. (xx, 159)

Both Huxley and Eliot, like the other scientists quoted, point to
a reality more complex than that which appears to the senses,
a reality constructed of hypotheses rather than certainties.

The point is not primarily one of influence, which is notor-
iously difficult to establish, but of intertextuality, a shared
discourse of the 1870s in which science became not so much
the 'dis-covery' of hitherto unknown 'facts' (a word which
Eliot herself tends to place in problematic quotation marks)
but the construction of new theories which enabled new connections to be made. Lewes and Eliot remained philosophical
realists, committed to a belief in an objective world to which
scientific theories pointed and by which they could be verified
or disproved. According to Lewes, the scientist's 'fictions' were
'moulded by the pressures of Reality' – one of the many deeply
significant nouns Lewes habitually capitalised (Problems I, 289)
– but they were no more transparent upon that reality than were
the novelist's fictions. In other words, Lewes, Eliot and their
scientific contemporaries had not altogether abandoned the

7

search for grand narratives, but were aware of their fragile and provisional status.

These epistemological problems will be discussed further in relation to the construction of character. Here it is important to recognise the self-consciously scientific discourse which pervades the novel, the repeated references to experiments, electric batteries, microscopes and so on. George Eliot referred to her fiction generally as 'experiments in life' (Letters V, 75), while the opening sentence of *Middlemarch* calls history the 'experiments of Time' (Prelude, 3). The narrator frequently refers to attempts to understand character and action in terms reminiscent of those employed to discuss the use and limits of the imagination in science:

> Even with a microscope directed on a water-drop we find ourselves making interpretations which turn out to be rather coarse; for whereas under a weak lens you may seem to see a creature exhibiting an active voracity into which other smaller creatures actively play as if they were so many animated tax-pennies, a stronger lens reveals to you certain tiniest hairlets which make vortices for these victims while the swallower waits passively at his receipt of custom. (vi, 49)

All depends upon the point of view. In another part of the novel a switch in narrative perspective is described in terms of an experiment in physics, the need to watch the effects of an electric battery 'at some distance from the point where the movement we were interested in was set up' (xl, 326). The narrative strategy of the whole novel could be said to be that advocated by Lydgate himself: 'there must be a systole and diastole in all inquiry,' he insists; 'a man's mind must be continually expanding and shrinking between the whole human horizon and the horizon of an object-glass' (lxiii, 524), between the way an individual perceives himself or herself and the way he or she appears to less interested observers.

There is a clear link between the development of such sophisticated scientific hypotheses, with their complicated critical (as opposed to naïve) realism, their recognition of the role of intermediary processes of perception between the individual and the external world, and the development of a more complex literary realism. The Ruskinian doctrine that 'all truth and beauty are to be attained by a humble and faithful study of nature', praised in Eliot's review of the third volume of *Modern Painters* (Essays, 266) and reiterated in Chapter 17 of *Adam Bede*, gives way in Eliot's later fiction to a more complex awareness of the distortions involved in all human perception. 'Reality' can only be understood relatively, in the terms of reference available at a particular point in time. This, in a way, is the subject of *Middlemarch*: the limitations imposed upon the individual by his and especially her insertion into history.

The limits imposed upon women at the time in which *Middlemarch* is set (and exposed in the intervening years before the time of writing) provide another important context in which the novel should be read (as it is in Chapter 5). The question of reform, particularly of the political system, is another key context, since the novel, which was written shortly after the Second Reform Bill, culminates in the First Reform Bill (discussed in Chapter 6). The whole question of history, which occupies much of Eliot's notebooks for the novel, and the contemporary critique of Christianity, both of which will be discussed at some length later in the book, provide other important contexts for the novel. It will have become apparent already that there is, in practice, no clear division between text and context. *Middlemarch* can be seen to share a number of discourses with other contemporary texts. To concentrate as I have done on its links with the scientific 'culture' of the period is simply to select one of the most striking departures of this novel from the traditional language of fiction – which many contemporary reviewers criticised – and to stress its importance for an understanding of Eliot's realism.

Eliot's realism, of course, can be related to other developments in nineteenth-century fiction. Because of her employment of a seemingly omniscient narrator to guide if not to control the reader's response, Eliot has been allied with Thackeray and Trollope, both of whom she read and admired. Like Thackeray's narrators, however, Eliot's can be shown to be less reliable, less certain, than is sometimes thought. As Wolfgang Iser has shown, the reader of *Vanity Fair* (1848) is encouraged to see through the illusions not only of the characters but also of the narrator. In realising (making actual what is implicit) the gulf between 'illusion' and 'reality' readers also bring into question their own ideology, their own understanding of the world. Thus the aim is not to project the author's view of objective reality upon the reader but 'to compel the reader ... to discover his [or her] own reality'.[10]

In one particular formal feature of narrative, her development of the technique of free indirect speech, Eliot can be seen to have developed this sophisticated, self-conscious understanding of 'reality' beyond any of her contemporaries. Hans Robert Jauss illustrates, in, *Toward an Aesthetic of Reception* (1982), the way in which free indirect speech functions as a device which forces readers to question their habitual responses, their own construction of reality. Flaubert's *Madame Bovary* (1856–7), for example, was misread as celebrating and sympathising with Emma's glorification of adultery through lack of familiarity with this convention. The defence counsel at his trial for offending public morals demonstrated that the sentences depicting Emma's excitement at her own image in the mirror (that of an adulteress) were not to be read as an 'objective statement of the narrator's' but rather 'a subjective opinion' of the character. The slide between the narrative voice and that of the character confronts readers with 'a new "opaque" reality' which they themselves must judge.[11]

Eliot, as we shall see, provokes her readers into a similar complex pondering of what 'really' is the case. Her narrative voice, too, oscillates between criticism of her characters and sympathy with them in the manner of a Browning monologue. A particularly interesting parallel with *Middlemarch* in its recognition of philosophical relativism through narrative form is Browning's long poem of 1868, *The Ring and the Book*, with its many different versions of the supposed 'facts' of the case. In an age in which consensus about objective reality is evaporating, literature turns from simple to multiple points of view, exploring the psychological motivation of necessarily subjective standpoints. In providing so many different perspectives upon events, both Eliot and Browning anticipate the multiple voices of modernist texts such as *The Waste Land*, *Ulysses* and *The Waves*.[12]

Middlemarch can also be seen to build upon the conventions of the Victorian multi-plot novel as developed by Dickens in *Bleak House* (1852–3), *Little Dorrit* (1855–7) and *Our Mutual Friend* (1864–5), the first of which advertises the complexity of its world by providing two narrators. Wilkie Collins too resorts to multiple narrators in order to unravel the mysteries of *The Woman in White* (1859–60) and *The Moonstone* (1868). The conventions of serialisation, which demand a constant switching from one strand of the narrative to the others, all of which need to be included in each episode, militate against a univocal understanding of any of these novels. The 'artistic imperative to impose coherence and structure' must battle against the 'diversity, difference and variety' of the subject matter.[13] This, together with the intertextual nature of the 'reality' which *Middlemarch* weaves, should alert readers to the dangers of accepting too simple and too unified a model of its world.

Critical Reception of the Text

Eliot's contemporaries certainly found *Middlemarch* difficult, struggling to impose unity and coherence upon a text which veers in tone from the earnestly moralistic to the savagely sarcastic to the benignly humorous. More recent critics remain similarly baffled, unsure precisely how to respond: one 1987 study of *Middlemarch* complains of 'her absolute lack of any sense of the comic',[1] while another offers a whole chapter on 'Making Room for the Comic Spirit', celebrating Eliot's comic tolerance of what may be imperfect but cannot be changed.[2] Ladislaw, it should be noted, along with Mary Garth and Fred Vincy, is forever laughing, while Casaubon and Rosamond's inability to let go, their fear of being laughed at, reflects the rigid seriousness with which they take themselves. Lewes wrote to John Blackwood, the publisher of *Middlemarch*, of 'being in a perpetual gurgle of laughter' on re-reading the novel, receiving a reply full of gratitude for 'such glorious Tonics as Middlemarch'. Blackwood, who knew what Eliot wanted to hear, described how he had spent 'the greater part of the day reading, grinning and thinking as I read' (Letters V, 195 and 199). All readers of *Middlemarch* know that they are expected to think but many hesitate before grinning and gurgling.

The revolutionary format of the novel, which first appeared in eight half-volumes at intervals of two months, seems to have been designed to affect not only buying but reading habits, forcing readers not only to circumvent the libraries[3] but to become more circumspect themselves, slowing down to a thinking pace. Both Eliot and Lewes complained bitterly of inattentive readers who 'gulped down four volumes at a sitting' (Letters V, 257 and 264). Eliot responded to demand, however, taking careful note of Blackwood's comments, and revising the first three volumes to meet his characteristically Victorian concern with the central characters. He was 'disappointed', for example, not to find much news of his 'old friends' Dorothea and her family in the second part (Letters V, 167), so Eliot introduced more Middlemarchers into Part One in order to prepare readers better for the broadening of interest away from 'Miss Brooke', and transferred Chapters 19 to 22, portraying Dorothea in Rome, from their original position at the beginning of Part Three to the end of Part Two (Letters V, 184 and 224). Contemporary interest continued to focus upon Dorothea and the question of whether and whom she would marry after Casaubon's death, some of the dislike of the ending being the product of disappointed hopes that Lydgate would be the man.

What drew most fire from critics of the ending of the novel, however, were the passages in the penultimate paragraph – added at proof stage for inclusion in the first edition of the novel and removed from all subsequent editions – in which the blame for Dorothea's difficulties is placed firmly upon society:

> Among the many remarks passed on her mistakes, it was never said in the neighbourhood of Middlemarch that such mistakes could not have happened if the society into which she was born had not smiled on propositions of marriage from a sickly man to a girl less than half his own age – *on modes of education which make a woman's knowledge another name for motley ignorance – on rules of conduct which are in flat contradiction to its own loudly-asserted beliefs. While this is the social air which mortals begin to breathe*, there will be collisions such as those in Dorothea's life, where *great feelings will take the aspect of error, and great faith the aspect of illusion*. (Clarendon Finale, 824, my italics to represent what remained in later editions)

Many reviewers took offence at this passage, suggesting that Eliot exaggerated the sins of her society in order to protect the characters who embodied her own values. 'What more could Dorothea's friends have done,' asked the *Canadian Monthly*, 'unless they had put strychnine in Casaubon's tea?'[4]

Another complaint shared by many contemporary reviewers was that the book held out too little hope: 'the spiritual effect of her poems and stories', according to a *Spectator* article which appeared in the same month as the first issue of *Middlemarch*, 'is utterly, blankly melancholy' (Letters V, 296). Even friends such as Barbara Bodichon found the novel's wit and liveliness overshadowed by the 'coming misery' of its heroine, whom Bodichon likened to 'a child dancing into the quicksand on a sunny morning' (Letters IX, 33–4). Eliot herself had promised John Blackwood that there would be 'no unredeemed tragedy in the solution of the story' (Letters V, 296). She warned another friend to expect disappointment at the ending but then to look back at the Prelude, which would help to explain what happened (Letters V, 330). The novel was certainly not intended to produce 'the impression of black melancholy and despair' (Letters V, 261).

Nevertheless it did. *Scribner's Monthly* dwelt on the case of 'a sensitive and thoughtful young man, who rose from the perusal of *Middlemarch* with his eyes suffused with tears, exclaiming: "My God! and is that all?" '[5] Richard Hutton's many reviews of the novel focused on its rejection of the comforts of Christianity, doubting whether 'any one lays the book down without an extra twinge of melancholy'.[6] One of his reviews in the *Spectator* complained of Eliot taunting the world with credulity, for 'her melancholy scepticism is too apt to degenerate into scorn'.[7] Even Sidney Colvin's appreciative article in the *Fortnightly Review* ended by asking whether such painful realism could be altogether satisfactory as art: 'Is it that a literature, which confronts all the problems of life and the world, and recognises all the springs of action, and all that clogs those springs, ... must be like life itself, to leave us sad and hungry?'[8]

It is largely Eliot's 'pessimistic' philosophy that explains her loss of prestige and popularity from the 1890s until the end of the Second World War. The reaction against the Victorian reverence with which she had earlier been treated can be detected in W. E. Henley's label of 1890, 'George Sand *plus* Science and *minus* sex', which parodies Thomas Huxley's definition of her beloved Positivism as 'Catholicism *minus* Christianity'. George Saintsbury found too little frivolity or passion in her work, while Yeats and Shaw made similar complaints of an excess in analysis and a deficiency of hope.[9] Leslie Stephen, who found *Middlemarch* 'a rather painful book', blamed the increasing dominance of her philosophy for the loss of 'her early charm'.[10] Virginia Woolf, in spite of her recognition of the maturity of *Middlemarch*, shared her father's reservations. Such eminent literary figures as Oliver Elton, Edmund Gosse and David Cecil continued to present an unappetising picture of Eliot as an over-earnest, under-creative moralist.

It was a new generation of literary critics operating mainly in Cambridge in the years immediately after the Second World War who resurrected interest in Eliot and the Victorian values she represented: F. R. Leavis, V. S. Pritchett, Humphrey House, Basil Willey and Joan Bennett.[11] For Leavis it was her moral seriousness combined with her incomparable intellectual powers which produced the 'knowledge alive with understanding' so magnificently displayed in *Middlemarch*, particularly in its analysis of character. Leavis criticised Eliot's over-identification with Dorothea, which he saw as a product of her own immature 'soul-hunger', opening a long and unresolvable critical debate about the 'Theresa complex', the desire for martyrdom, from which both heroine and author have been said to suffer.[12] Interest at this time continued to focus either upon characterisation or intellectual 'background', although Joan Bennett tried to bridge the gap between Eliot's mind and her art, arguing that *Middlemarch* itself succeeded in fusing its intellectual brilliance and rich variety of detail into a coherent and aesthetically satisfying whole.[13]

The concern with form, a deliberate attempt to rebut Henry James's dismissal of *Middlemarch* as 'a treasure-house of detail, but ... an indifferent whole',[14] produced an impressive series of books in the late 1950s and early 1960s celebrating *The Art of George Eliot* (to use W. J. Harvey's 1961 title). Harvey's own survey of earlier criticism (in a collection of essays claiming that *Middlemarch* was generally regarded as 'the greatest English novel') explicitly contrasts the Victorian concern with character and ideas with the 'modern concern more with form'.[15] The greatness of *Middlemarch*, he claims in his 1965 Introduction to the Penguin edition of the novel, 'lies in its overall design', in the unity and coherence achieved 'by the poise of the omniscient author controlling the action'.[16] David Daiches' 1963 survey of the novel ends with similar praise of 'the firm control that the author had over her material'.[17]

By the 1970s, of course, such 'control' had once more become a liability. Graham Martin's Introduction to *Middlemarch* for Open University students in 1974 alerts them to the danger of Eliot's 'over-controlling the characters' and being too heavy-handedly explicit in authorial commentary.[18] By then, literary criticism had begun to change dramatically in response to continental theory, in particular the structuralist focus upon language and its ideological construction of 'reality' (the way in which all cultural codes necessarily embody a society's beliefs and prejudices about the world). *Middlemarch*, from being the culmination of a great tradition of English realism, had become an objectionable example of the classic realist text, whose defining feature, according to Colin MacCabe, was the dominance of the narrative voice over all the other discourses in the novel, as if the author had privileged access to a self-evident reality upon which her language was totally transparent.[19]

Eliot's creative process seemed also to fit Roland Barthes' characterisation of the process by which the classic realist text comes into being: the author first conceives a fixed and static signified before finding appropriate signifiers to express that meaning. The critic reverses the process, returning triumphantly to the original meaning, forming a closed circle of closely controlled interpretation.[20] Hillis Miller objected in similar fashion to the distinction implied by the metaphors within the novel between 'optic' (how things are seen objectively by the narrator) and 'semiotic' (how they are interpreted by the characters). For Miller all seeing involves interpretation, including that of the narrator, who is falsely accorded a metalanguage which is transparent upon the world.[21]

These objections, whatever validity they have for particular passages in the novel, were themselves made to appear too reductive by the increasingly sophisticated critics of the 1980s, who were alerted by deconstructive techniques to the tensions and contradictions running through all texts. 'It is precisely because the narrator's discourse is never entirely unambiguous, predictable, and in total control of the other discourses,' according to David Lodge, 'that the novel survives, to be read and re-read, without ever being finally closed or exhausted.'[22] In the following section I will attempt to indicate some of the ways in which post-structuralist critical perspectives have opened up the text of *Middlemarch*, unravelling its many strands of meaning and releasing the dialogue of voices, the play of language, to be found within it.

Theoretical Perspectives

Some critics would deny any objective status to the text. Stanley Fish, for example, argues that it is the interpretive strategy that creates the text rather than the text dictating a particular response.[1] Wolfgang Iser invests the text, the marks on the page, with more control over the way in which its readers 'actualise' it, bringing into being that mental 'object' which is the literary work.[2] It is clear enough from the preceding history of the reception of *Middlemarch* that the different questions and assumptions which different critics bring to the text 'dis-cover' certain previously 'invisible' aspects of the text. It should come as no surprise, then, that what emerges from a post-modern, post-structuralist reading of *Middlemarch* is a post-modern, post-structuralist novel, full of gaps, absences, tensions and contradictions, a self-conscious probing of the governing assumptions of Western civilization: truth, presence (of God and the self), history, fact, origin and gender.

To some extent, as I acknowledged in the Preface, such a reading is partial and anachronistic, ignoring those features of the novel which are characteristically 'modern' in their search for truth and unity. I will try to maintain the notion of 'double reading' which does justice to the modern context in which *Middlemarch* was written as well as the post-modern context in which it is being read. I will try to establish the frameworks of belief within which Eliot was working, the discourses she adopted from contemporary scientists, theologians, sociologists

18

and feminists, as well as the seeds of their disruption which she sows. For post-structuralist strategies of reading, I would argue, locate tensions, contradictions and questions which are 'there' in the text. To apply such strategies to *Middlemarch* should also serve to illustrate and to test these theories, bringing out the differences they make in critical practice, highlighting aspects of the text which earlier critical approaches failed to notice. It might be 'more democratic to study *Coronation Street* than *Middlemarch*', as a contributor to *Re-Reading English* (1982) recognised, but it is also necessary to show that canonical texts may not be what they had previously seemed.[3]

Earlier critics, for example, saw the narrator as imposing an authoritative and coherent vision of the world upon the text. But recent writers, building upon the work of Bakhtin, have come to recognise the 'polyphonic' play of different voices in prose fiction, a 'heteroglossia' in which no single discourse is given priority.[4] For Bakhtin these voices seem to have represented separate consciousnesses, but later critics such as Kristeva have applied his principle to tensions within the same voice, in particular within the narrator.[5] In *Middlemarch*, as we shall see, the narrative tone is particularly hard to gauge, oscillating as it does between ironic echoing and subversion of the attitudes of the characters and their society. The language of the characters mixes with that of the narrator, who sometimes adopts a prosaic commonsense pose similar to that of conservative Middlemarch, and at other times pleads in tragic or epic terms for a fuller understanding of the characters. This mixture of prophetic and prosaic voices, which baffled contemporaries, delights modern critics, affording multiple opportunities to analyse the complexities of Eliot's language, as I will do in Chapter 1 of my 'Reading of the Text', in the second part of this book.

For many earlier critics, as we have seen, the main interest in *Middlemarch* lay in the development and analysis of character. Serialisation, as in soap opera, encouraged contemporary readers of the novel to treat the characters as 'old friends' whose ongoing lives they could continue to follow through successive episodes. Even the revaluation of Eliot initiated by Leavis and others tended to focus on how well Lydgate was 'done' and how 'real' he was in comparison with Ladislaw, who was 'not substantially (everyone agrees) "there"'.[6] Dorothea's second husband has not been without his defenders but they too tend to treat the young man as a real person, dwelling on his student days supposedly outside the text and even in one case claiming that 'Dorothea invents no fiction about Ladislaw nor he about her'.[7]

But that is precisely what *Middlemarch* is: fiction. And fiction draws attention to the processes of characterisation, showing *how* character is constructed. Ladislaw, like Balzac's Sarrasine, so fully analysed by Barthes, is a figure not a person, 'an impersonal network of symbols' for the reader to dwell upon.[8] What is particularly interesting about *Middlemarch*, as I hope to show in Chapter 2, is the way in which characters are explicitly presented as clusters of signs for their neighbours to interpret. The text itself alerts us to the ideological construction of character, to the way in which characters see themselves and others through the distortions of desire and prejudice. While lending itself in this respect to psychoanalytic interpretation, encouraging readers to invest characters with subconscious as well as conscious desires, *Middlemarch* displays the constructed fictional status of all characterisation.

Another traditional area of concern has been the intellectual 'background' to Eliot's writing. So meticulous was her reading of philosophy, theology and science, reflected in her careful translation of Spinoza, Strauss and Feuerbach and in her detailed annotations of many others, that it is easy to trace the 'influence' of these thinkers upon her work. But literary influence, as Harold Bloom has shown, is rarely a matter of the benign transmission of ideas; more often, as with Eliot, it is an interpretive struggle to differentiate her position from those of her precursors.[9] Intensive study of the notebooks and quarries for *Middlemarch* has confirmed that they functioned not as blueprints for the novel but as part of a more complex creative process in which ideas would 'simmer' in Eliot's mind before achieving final expression.[10] The sharing of discourse between *Middlemarch* and contemporary scientific accounts of the world has already been discussed, and a similar intertextuality with historians and theologians will emerge in Chapters 3 and 4. All writing, of course, is necessarily composed of other people's language, subtly transformed by its new context, but this process is particularly evident in *Middlemarch*.

All the theoretical perspectives so far discussed have been concerned with textual analysis. The final two chapters of this book, however, consider more controversial political and ideological questions of the kind raised by feminist and Marxist critics. Feminists have found Eliot especially difficult to appropriate because she seems so readily to have accepted the patriarchal values of her time. Even her choice of a male pseudonym seems to place her in what Elaine Showalter has called the 'feminine' phase (ending significantly in 1880, the year of her death), during which women writers simply attempted to emulate the achievements of the dominant masculine culture, internalising many of its assumptions about women and their role in society.[11] Many feminist critics are angry with George Eliot for not allowing Dorothea to do what she herself did, that is, to escape the restrictions imposed upon women by becoming an independent professional writer living with her lover beyond the conventions of marriage.[12] Others argue that Eliot represses her anger at patriarchal attitudes, advocating a dangerously submissive ethic of self-sacrifice and resignation to unchangeable evils. Her critique of male chauvinism in *Middlemarch*, however, to be explored in Chapter 5, is extremely powerful, as is her analysis of conventional gender construction in Rosamond Vincy. Even the limits imposed upon Dorothea can also be read more as a reflection of the conditions of the 1830s than as an acceptance of patriarchy.

Marxist critics share a similar ambivalence towards *Middlemarch*, which subverts provincial conservatism as savagely as male chauvinism. Nobody shows more clearly than Eliot the way ideology in Althusser's sense inserts individuals into history, constructing a self-consciousness which only appears to be freely chosen. *Middlemarch* also analyses the processes of change and the difficulties of introducing constitutional, medical and educational reform. It portrays the ways in which class, money and power operate within a capitalist society. All this, as will become apparent in the last chapter of the book, is brought into the open by Marxist critics, who tend nevertheless to dislike what they see as Eliot's displacement of politics to the margins of the text and its reduction finally to a matter of personal morality.[13] Their objections to *Middlemarch* echo Marx's own rejection of Feuerbach as too idealistic, insufficiently grounded in material reality.[14] My own analysis of the social and political dimensions of the novel, however, suggests that such material practices as the exercise of wealth, rank and power are all clearly displayed. I will be concerned to explore the depth and complexity of the problems Eliot exposes rather than the limits of her implied solutions. *Middlemarch*, I want to suggest, is a novel to be valued more for its questions than its answers.

II

Middlemarch
A Reading of the Text

1

The Play of Voices

Middlemarch, like all novels, is constructed of language which thus becomes an object of critical attention. But *Middlemarch*, more than most other novels, is about language, about dialogue, about the attempt to communicate and the difficulty of undistorted representation of the world. Even the omniscient and ubiquitous narrative voice is not a monologue, a metalanguage imposing a single vision of reality upon all other voices within the text, but a dialogue, a palimpsest, a web woven of different discourses whose many-layered ironies require careful disentangling by the reader upon whom falls the ultimate responsibility of constructing meaning. This particular metaphor of the web, which appears in a variety of forms throughout the text, underlines the point made explicit by the narrator: 'we all of us ... get our thoughts entangled in metaphors, and act fatally on the strength of them' (x, 70). The fictional world of *Middlemarch*, like the linguistic worlds we all inhabit, is woven of metaphor, our main resource for making connections.

Language becomes the subject of discussion at a number of points in the novel. Rosamond, for example, finds fault with her mother's 'vulgar' expressions, only to have her notions of 'correct' English ridiculed by her irreverent brother as 'the slang of prigs who write history and essays'. His suggested game, in which she would have to identify the 'bits of slang and poetry' copied by him onto separate slips of paper (xi, 81), illustrates the importance of register – that it is context which determines appropriateness of language. Even Mrs Garth, regarded by her husband as 'a treasury of correct language', allows her son's 'inappropriate language to pass without correction' in the context of extreme emotion: he is allowed to leap about the room celebrating the fact that his sister is an 'old brick' for volunteering to make good her parents' financial loss by teaching at a school (xl, 328).

Mrs Garth's normal view of language is brusque and business-like, for she believes in its power to impose order upon the chaos of experience. 'In a general wreck of society', we are told, she 'would have tried to hold her Lindley Murray above the waves'. She explains to her recalcitrant son Ben, who hates grammar and fails to see its use, that 'correct' language avoids misunderstanding. Without a knowledge of grammar, she insists, 'You would use wrong words, and put words in the wrong places, and instead of making people understand you, they would turn away from you as a tiresome person.' This, of course, is precisely what her pedantry causes her son to do to her, as he threatens to 'leave off' talking altogether (xxiv, 202). Communication turns out not to be quite as straightforward as Mrs Garth thinks.

It is the variety and flexibility of language that appeals to the romantic young Ladislaw, comforting himself for being told by Naumann that he cannot paint. Language, he insists, is a 'finer medium' of representation than the plastic arts, providing a 'fuller image, which is all the better for being vague'. While painting is limited to the external representation of his beloved Dorothea, language can 'paint her voice', her divinest essence (xix, 156–7). He will tell her later on in the novel that she herself is a poem, which alerts the reader to the fact that what Ladislaw loves in her is at least in part his own creation.

The trouble with language, as Lydgate realises, is that it often becomes a screen, a barrier to understanding rather than a window onto the world. His 'moment of vocation' involves a defamiliarisation, a sudden awareness of the inadequacy of his former conceptions about the body and its functions. What he reads under 'anatomy' in his uncle's encyclopaedia overturns his whole view of life. The metaphor of a valve or folding door in the heart acts as a 'crevice' through which a startling new light is shed upon the mechanisms of the human body: 'the world was made new to him by a presentiment of endless processes filling the vast spaces planked out of his sight by that wordy ignorance that he had supposed to be knowledge' (xv, 118). This complex metaphor makes language so opaque as to be a barrier to knowledge, a covering over of the complex processes which new terms can begin to uncover.

Whether language can ever become transparent upon the world begins to appear unlikely. New metaphors merely make the world anew, constructing a different set of paradigms for its decoding (or rather re-encoding, since there is no possibility of escaping the need for some set of codes, some framework of perception). Mrs Bulstrode certainly regards fine language as a 'noble drapery' to throw over unpleasant reality (xxxi, 245), while her niece Rosamond fails to see that it is the language of conventional romance which constructs her distorted image of Lydgate. What she calls 'falling in love' is displayed as the product of a 'romance' woven from her own fantasy. It is a 'result' which she has 'contemplated beforehand', dwelling on the arrival of a tall, dark, handsome and well-connected stranger. For 'a stranger', we are told, 'was absolutely necessary to Rosamond's social romance'. 'Reality' comes to mirror her desires, making it only 'natural' that Lydgate should return her love (xii, 96).

This process of naturalisation, by which we appropriate the world, reducing it to the dimensions of our words, making the strange familiar and the frightening tame, is evident in the many different types of discourse which appear in *Middlemarch*. Rosamond's father, for example, finds comfort in the 'felicitous word "demise".... Considered as a demise, old Featherstone's death assumed a merely legal aspect, so that Mr Vincy could tap his snuff-box over it and be jovial' (xxxi, 248). 'Demise' is one of the many terms adopted so inappropriately by Bulstrode in producing the document required of Fred Vincy by Mr Featherstone (xiv, 109). All Bulstrode's terms, in fact, especially his religious cant, require translation. 'A useful member' of the board of the Fever Hospital is 'defined as one who would originate nothing, and always vote with Mr Bulstrode' (xliv, 371). 'What is called being apostolic now', Lydgate explains to Dorothea, 'is an impatience of everything in which the parson doesn't cut the principal figure' (l, 405). Language, once again, is seen to distort the world, or rather to enable us to construct it in our own image.

Other discourses represented in *Middlemarch* include academic, political and medical jargon (jargon being the inappropriate use of specialised terms). One of the problems from which Casaubon suffers is his inability to escape from the academic register: 'he had not two styles of talking at his command' (iii, 21). He talks and writes to Dorothea, therefore, as if she were a lecture audience, carefully glossing his Greek and Latin phrases but making no other concessions to her ignorance or individuality. His letter of proposal is notorious for its pomposity, its author allowing himself only 'such activity of the affections as even the preoccupations of a work too special to be abdicated could not uninterruptedly dissimulate' (v, 35). This is hardly the language of passion. The 'frigid rhetoric' of his speech on her acceptance is likened by the narrator to 'the cawing of an amorous rook' (v, 41). The language of the lecture-room is clearly inadequate for love.

Political rhetoric is portrayed as even more distorted, for instance in the praise heaped by the *Pioneer* upon Mr Brooke as one of those

> men whose minds had from long experience acquired breadth as well as concentration, decision of judgment as well as tolerance, dispassionateness as well as energy – in fact, all those qualities which in the melancholy experience of mankind have been the least disposed to share lodgings. (xxxvii, 293–4)

Brooke's patronising benevolence certainly cuts little ice with his tenant Dagley, who resents being addressed as 'my good fellow'. ' "Oh, ay, I'm a good feller, am I?" ' he repeats 'with a loud snarling irony' (xxxix, 324). Brooke observes that his tenant has been 'dining' (i.e. drinking) heavily and tries to appease him. But Dagley is determined to 'have his say', letting him know precisely what 'Rinform' means for idle landlords. Eliot resorts constantly to inverted commas within the narrative voice to indicate the special terminology the two men use, to capture as precisely as possible the class barriers inscribed in language.

Middlemarch in general resents unfamiliar language, whether in religion, politics, art or medicine, so that Lydgate's ideas are described 'in point of fact' (always a dangerous word in this novel) as 'flighty, foreign notions' (xxvi, 216). A town which has grown accustomed to 'squitchineal' and 'soopling' rejects such concepts as the 'expectant method' which Lydgate ill-advisedly explains to the loquacious Mr Trumbull. Gossip encounters science and their dissonant play of voices, their struggle for power over the minds of Middlemarch, grows increasingly absurd. The auctioneer profits from his illness by 'learning many new words which seemed suited to the dignity of his secretions', words that he is soon parroting to his neighbours and thereby adding weight to their suspicions of the new doctor's charlatanism (xlv, 368–9).

If, as Solomon Waule observes, 'Auctioneers talk wild', attempting to sell goods at a higher rate than they merit, sincerity seems almost to require the abandonment of language altogether. Caleb Garth is bedevilled by 'a sense that words were scantier than thoughts' (xl, 332). He responds to music with gestures rather than words, 'throwing much unutterable language into his outstretched hands' (lvi, 450–1). When his wife tries to probe his reasons for resigning all Bulstrode's business he replies with a monosyllabic grunt and a wave of the hand which she recognises as 'a sign of his not intending to speak further on the subject' (lxix, 570). In the light of young Ben's similar desire to 'leave off' language and the breakdown of communication in so many of the marriages in the novel, *Middlemarch* has been called 'a masterpiece of interrupted dialectics, of dialogues broken off'.[1] If language is supposed to be a mode of interactive communication, it manifestly fails.

One of the most brilliant aspects of *Middlemarch*, however, is the way it captures the implications and indirectness of spoken dialogue. Take, for example, the way Mrs Bulstrode's friends convey their sympathetic awareness of her husband's downfall without communicating any of the details of which she remains ignorant:

> 'I am sure I should be glad that you always should live at Middlemarch, Mrs Bulstrode,' said Mrs Hackbutt, with a slight sigh. 'Still, we must learn to resign ourselves, wherever our lot may be cast. Though I am sure there will always be people in this town who will wish you well.'

Mrs Bulstrode is left to guess what it is that lies 'behind this speech', mysteriously referred to without being named. Mrs Plymdale is similarly indirect, although her promise 'never to turn her back on her friends' convinces Mrs Bulstrode that 'what had happened must be some kind of misfortune'. She finds herself unable, however, to ask a direct question, hurrying away 'before she had heard anything explicit' (lxxiv, 612–13). The ideal of language as a vehicle for truth succumbs once more to the realities of its practice as a means of wielding power over others.

Casaubon attempts to intimidate Dorothea by similar indirectness. The first time she attempts to raise the subject of Ladislaw in Rome he announces, 'I met him outside, and we made our final adieux, I believe.' The second time he responds with frosty politeness, 'What is that, my love?' The narrator explains that 'he always said "my love" when his manner was the coldest'. It is a tribute to Dorothea's courage (and naïvety?) that he is forced finally into an explicit closing of the subject: 'I had a duty towards him. ... The young man, I confess, is not otherwise an object of interest to me, nor need we, I think, discuss his future course.' The chapter ends with the terse statement that 'Dorothea did not mention Will again' (xxii, 184–5). She is forced into a silence fraught with repressed criticism.

A more comic example of conversational implicature (the unspoken rules governing the way we speak and listen to each other) also involves Dorothea. It occurs in the opening chapter of the novel when she diverts her sister's suggestion that they look at their late mother's jewels by focusing on the way in which Celia justifies her request, that it is six months since their uncle gave them to her: 'What a wonderful little almanac you are' (i, 10). Dorothea's flouting of the conversational principle of cooperation, her failure to assume that her sister is conveying something relevant, has been shown to point behind the surface dialogue to the 'major conflicts within her which are the subject of the entire novel' – conflicts between her repressed sexuality and her compulsion towards self-sacrifice which will be explored more fully later in the book.[2]

There is a perpetual conflict, too, between what Rosamond says and what she thinks. ' "Of course, she is devoted to her husband," ' she says of Dorothea, 'thinking at the same time that it was not so very melancholy to be mistress of Lowick Hall, with a husband likely to die soon. "Do you think her very handsome?" ' The implied train of thought reveals how her mind really works, in spite of the propriety of her speech, as it does when she resists her aunt's reprimand for allowing Lydgate's attentions without gaining any commitment on his part: ' "The town's talk is of very little consequence, I think," said Rosamond, inwardly gratified'. Aunt Bulstrode is forced to defend her niece's action in entertaining strangers by citing the example of Abraham and Moses, only to be told by the exasperated Mrs Plymdale, 'I was not speaking in a religious sense, Harriet. I spoke as a mother' (xxxi, 241–3). Middlemarch, it is clear, operates within very restricted registers, confining its religion within the walls of its churches where it is not allowed to influence the everyday world.

It is not only between characters, however, that the dialogue of *Middlemarch* takes place. There is a constant dialogue between the wise, avuncular narrator and the reader, a conversation in which the narrator ('I') gradually attempts to persuade the reader ('you') of certain truths about the human condition (what 'we' are like).[3] 'We are all of us born in moral stupidity,' announces this authoritative narrator, 'taking the world as an udder to feed our supreme selves' (xxi, 173). Many readers shy away from such overt didacticism, rebelling against 'the voice of the wise woman'.[4] For others, however, this dialogue is the way Eliot involves her readers in the world of the novel: 'The meaning of *Middlemarch* lies in the implicit conversation between that narrator and the reader, ... its discursive as opposed to its dramatic plot.'[5] What is learnt in the process of reading emerges from this dialogue.

It is important, however, to recognise that the narrative voice in *Middlemarch* varies greatly. To divide the text of the novel into mimesis (the representation of reported speech and action) and diegesis (the narrator's commentary upon these) is too simple; the novel dissolves these boundaries in complex layers of irony.[6] At times the narrative voice echoes the complacent voice of conservative provincial England in mock dismissal of the lofty aspirations of the characters; at other times it pleads for them with solemn sympathy.[7] The use of epigraphs adds even more voices to the text, creating 'a "polyphony", a multiplicity of truths, an endless oscillation between incompatible positions'.[8]

The difficult role of the reader in steering a path between these often ironic voices emerges most clearly in response to the technique of free indirect speech, in which diegesis and mimesis, the language of the narrator and that of the character, mix almost inseparably.[9] The levels of irony surrounding the clash between Dorothea's aspirations on the one hand, and the commonsense attitudes of Middlemarch on the other, are a case in point. On the surface the following paragraph from the opening chapter of the novel represents the narrow provincial attitudes of the voice of Middlemarch:

> And how should Dorothea not marry? – a girl so handsome and with such prospects? Nothing could hinder it but her love of extremes, and her insistence on regulating life according to notions which might cause a wary man to hesitate before he made her an offer, or even might lead her at last to refuse all offers. A young lady of some birth and fortune, who knelt suddenly down on a brick floor by the side of a sick labourer and prayed fervidly as if she thought herself living in the time of the Apostles – who had strange whims of fasting like a Papist, and

of sitting up at night to read old theological books! Such a wife might awaken you some fine morning with a new scheme for the application of her income which would interfere with political economy and the keeping of saddle-horses: a man would naturally think twice before he risked himself in such fellowship. Women were expected to have weak opinions; but the great safeguard of society and of domestic life was, that opinions were not acted on. Sane people did what their neighbours did, so that if any lunatics were at large, one might know and avoid them. (i, 8–9)

As the paragraph develops, in fact, the voice appears to become more dominantly male, with its suspicion of the kind of ardour which interferes with masculine comforts. And yet the reader, who soon learns not to accept Celia's dismissal of her sister's 'notions', also becomes aware of the fact that Dorothea does indeed suffer from a 'love of extremes', has been affected by evangelical demands for apostolic zeal, does dream up impractical utopian schemes and does select the most unsuitable husband. She will need reminding by Mrs Cadwallader after Casaubon's death that 'we have all got to exert ourselves a little to keep sane, and call things by the same names as other people call them by'. She cannot always be 'playing tragedy queen and taking things sublimely'. Dorothea, of course, objects that she has never called things by the same name as her neighbours, to be told that she has since learnt from her mistake. 'I still think that the greater part of the world is mistaken about many things', she maintains and the debate remains unresolved (liv, 438–9). In other words, there is a double irony here: the narrator distances herself/himself both from the prejudices of Middlemarch and from Dorothea's naïve ardour.

The double-edged tone with which Dorothea is treated in the opening chapter continues throughout the book. Her over-estimation of Casaubon, for example, reflects both an admirable rejection of conventional Middlemarch attitudes and an absurdly uncritical idealism. In her desire to go 'beyond the shallows of ladies'-school literature' she sees 'a living Bossuet' in the pedantic rector, 'a modern Augustine' (iii, 23). The irony of her feeling that to marry this man 'would be like marrying Pascal' is immediately undercut by the admirable ambition she has 'to lead a grand life here – now – in England' (iii, 24). Readers who have laughed too readily at her simplicity find themselves too quickly identified with the narrowness of Middlemarch.

There is a similar ambivalence about the portrait of the two sisters in Chapter 4. Celia, who shaɾeᴅ her neighbours' suspicions of Dorothea's 'notions', nevertheless notices the way her sister fails to see what is 'quite plain' to everyone else. It is Celia who punctures Dorothea's patronising description of Sir James Chettam as a ' "good creature, and more sensible than anyone would imagine" ' with the straightforward interpretation, ' "You mean that he appears silly." ' But then Celia reveals her limitations by describing her sister's designs of improved cottages as a 'fad', provoking further outbursts from Dorothea on the impossibility of doing 'anything nobly Christian, living among people with such petty thoughts' (iv, 29–31). The irony here cuts both ways: Dorothea is presented as both admirable and mistaken, Celia as a model of commonsense (both common and sensible).

The oscillation of irony and sympathy in the presentation of Dorothea continues when she finds no support from Casaubon for these social projects:

> how could she be confident that one-roomed cottages were not for the glory of God, when men who knew the classics appeared to conciliate indifference to the cottages with zeal for the glory? Perhaps even Hebrew might be necessary – at least the alphabet and a few roots – in order to arrive at the core of things, and judge soundly on the social duties of the Christian. And she had not reached that point of renunciation at which she would have been satisfied with having a wise husband: she wished, poor child, to be wise herself. Miss Brooke was certainly very naive, with all her alleged cleverness. Celia, whose mind had never been thought too powerful, saw the emptiness of other people's pretensions much more readily. To have in general but little feeling seems to be the only security against feeling too much on any particular occasion. (vii, 52–3)

Here the narrator is overtly critical of Dorothea, of her naïvety, her idealisation of Casaubon and her tendency to extremes of feeling. But the overall effect of this passage is one of sympathy with her diffident self-questioning, her intense respect and desire for knowledge (in spite of being a woman), her social conscience and her spiritual ardour. The irony operates much more powerfully against the prejudices and limitations of her society. The process of unravelling these ironies teaches readers not to take anything the narrator says at face value.

Fred Vincy learns a similar lesson among the local horse-dealers. Horrock, for example, plays an extremely effective part in their dialogue by remaining silent throughout, forcing Fred all the while to speculate on his inner thoughts. Fred feels that he is beginning to understand this world, interpreting Bambridge's running down of a horse as a clear indication of his actual admiration and interest in the animal:

> every one who looked at the animal – even Horrock – was evidently impressed with its merit. To get all the advantage of being with men of this sort, you must know how to draw your inferences, and not be a spoon who takes things literally. (xxiii, 197)

Fred is clearly misreading the situation, which makes his confident pronouncements so ironic. Everything, however, is implicit: it is the reader who has to identify Fred's voice in the discourse, overlaid though it is with the slang of the fast set to which he is trying to belong.

Rosamond's voice has also to be identified in the passages of free indirect speech relating to her, for instance in her self-justification at secretly contacting Lydgate's relatives:

> there was but one person in Rosamond's world whom she did not regard as blameworthy, and that was the graceful creature with blond plaits and with little hands crossed before her, who had never expressed herself unbecomingly, and had always acted for the best – the best naturally being what she best liked. (lxv, 544)

The narrator cannot resist the temptation to gloss Rosamond's favourite phrase in this final sentence, clarifying the position for the reader, who must learn to make similar judgements about other characters with less assistance from the narrator.

Middlemarch, then, comprises a mixture of voices playing a variety of language-games to be identified and assessed by the reader. Running through the text, as has often been shown,[10] is a range of metaphors which help to establish motifs within the novel by weaving identifiable thematic patterns. This is one of the ways in which Eliot has been said to stamp a relatively stable and unified moral vision upon the novel. Metaphors of mirrors, for example, reflect the distorted perception and egoism of some characters in contrast with the relatively clear windows through which others perceive the world. Dorothea's illusory picture of Casaubon is described as a reflection in 'the ungauged reservoir' of his mind of 'every quality she herself brought' (iii, 20). But it becomes a characteristic activity on her part to look out of windows away from her own sorrows to identify the needs of others.

Mary Garth's eyes, too, are likened to 'clear windows where observation sat laughingly' (xiv, 114). Rosamond, in contrast, who is always preening herself before a mirror, fails to perceive any of her husband's qualities, causing Lydgate 'to look through less and less of interfering illusion at the blank, un-reflecting surface her mind presented to his ardour for the more impersonal ends of his profession' (lviii, 478). Bulstrode, who sees 'a very unsatisfactory reflection of himself in the coarse unflattering mirror' of Mr Vincy's mind (xiii, 108), later comes to wish that he could escape from himself, particularly from his past:

> he felt the scenes of his earlier life coming between him and everything else, as obstinately as when we look through the window from a lighted room, the objects we turn our backs on are still before us, instead of the grass and the trees. (lxi, 502)

Each of these examples varies the terms of the metaphor; the assumption that it is ever possible to interpret undistortedly, as if observing the world through a window, is brought into question by the manifest failure of so many of the characters to do so. If even Dorothea has a tendency to see her own reflection in others, how can anyone be certain of what he or she sees? Are not all the patterns to be found in the pier-glass equally doubtful? *Middlemarch* raises these unanswerable epistemological questions at the same time as providing standard liberal humanist answers about the moral preferability of altruism over egoism.[11]

A similar tension between stable and indeterminate meaning arises when these window/mirror metaphors merge with the more general images of light and darkness which pervade the novel. Casaubon's research, for example, is constantly depicted as a groping in the dark:

> Poor Mr Casaubon himself was lost among small closets and winding stairs, and in an agitated dimness about the Cabeiri, or in an exposure of other mythologists' ill-considered parallels, easily lost sight of any purpose which had prompted him to these labours. With his taper stuck before him he forgot the absence of windows, and in bitter manuscript remarks on other men's notions about the solar deities, he had become indifferent to the sunlight. (xx, 162)

His cousin, in contrast, is forever associated with sunshine and brightness. His hair seems 'to shake out light' when he turns his head, causing people to detect 'decided genius in this coruscation. Mr Casaubon, on the contrary, stood rayless' (xxi, 171). In whose eyes, the reader is forced to ask? The paragraph begins with Casaubon's perspective before becoming impersonal third-person narrative. The next sentence describes Dorothea's eyes 'turned anxiously on her husband'. Once again, the epistemological questions and the uncertainty of the narrative voice cloud the clarity of the moral judgement.

Casaubon certainly appears to Ladislaw as a monstrous figure, a minotaur luring innocent victims such as Dorothea into his gloomy cave. Even the maid calls his library 'a caticom', a veritable prison for his persecuted martyr-wife (xlviii, 393). When Ladislaw's mission of rescue to Lowick church fails, Dorothea seems doomed to perpetual darkness:

> She longed for work which would be directly beneficent like the

sunshine and the rain, and now it appeared that she was to live more and more in a virtual tomb, where there was the apparatus of a ghastly labour producing what would never see the light. (xlviii, 388–9)

It is Casaubon, however, who is finally entombed while Dorothea emerges from his shadow to enjoy Ladislaw's fertile light and rain.

It is impossible, of course, to fix metaphorical meaning or to halt the endless generation of new images. In the last example, light is seen to mix with rain to produce genuine creativity in contrast to the stillborn labour of Lowick Manor. Images of stagnant as opposed to running water, as we shall see, recur throughout Dorothea's marriage to Casaubon to indicate an absence of the energy, fertility and creativity which Ladislaw will provide. Other metaphorical clusters will be explored later, such as the multiple references to maiming, which dramatise the necessity of resignation to what cannot be changed. These metaphorical patterns, however, the staple diet of traditional criticism, should not be seen so much as imposing a fixed and univocal unity upon the novel as allowing readers to make connections, to follow through similarities, to recognise differences and so to produce a reading performance of the rich play of voices to be discovered within the text. No single reading can hope to be 'complete', as if reproducing a tapestry by following a design. Such spatial metaphors falsify the process of reading, neglecting both its temporal dimension and its context (which will always change). The very richness of metaphor in *Middlemarch*, along with the complexity of its analysis of language, preserves an element of play, allowing a certain freedom of interpretation.

2

The Construction of Character

Character has been called an invention of the Victorian realist novel, a rhetorical device to concentrate and clarify the enormous complexity of experience by creating coherent entities with whom readers can identify (having no such coherent identity themselves) and in whose meaningful stories they can find consolation for the meaninglessness of their own lives.[1] The construction of character in fiction both reflects and provokes a culture's understanding of the self. *Middlemarch* can be said self-consciously to dramatise this process since its characters are constantly misreading the signs they see in each other and constructing illusory portraits which are the product of their own desires. 'For images', in the words of the narrator, 'are the brood of desire' (xxxiv, 266). The inhabitants of Middlemarch are also shown to construct illusory images of themselves, repressing what they refuse to recognise as part of their psychological make-up. Dorothea, who is portrayed as gradually coming to some recognition of the sensual side of her nature, has been taken to exemplify Foucault's view that Victorian culture enshrined sexual passion as the 'secret' of identity, 'enjoining individuals to seek out and define the dangerous, primal "truth" of the sexuality buried within themselves'.[2] Her growth into self-consciousness provides one of the central fictions of the book. There is, from a post-modern perspective, no escape from fiction; only some fictions are more illusory and less self-critical than others.

Middlemarch, although it cannot be said to anticipate such radical deconstruction of character as self-conscious presence, does give explicit recognition to the process by which our perception of character is constructed, the way in which a coherent image both of the self and of others is built. A reflection upon changing social status in provincial society notices that even the 'few personages or families that stood with rocky firmness amid all this fluctuation, were slowly presenting new aspects in spite of solidity, and altering with the double change of self and beholder' (xi, 78). Character, in other words, is a combination of external and internal factors, of how we are seen and what we make of ourselves. 'Character', observes the narrator apropos of Lydgate's youthful promise, 'is a process and an unfolding. The man was still in the making ... and there were both virtues and faults capable of shrinking or expanding' (xv, 123). 'Character is not cut in marble,' as Farebrother says when ugly rumours spread about the doctor's dependence upon Bulstrode, 'it is not something solid and unalterable. It is something living and changing, and may become diseased as our bodies do' (lxxii, 602). The novel charts the complex construction of Lydgate's character both in the minds of others and in terms of his own self-perception.

Like many of the characters in the novel, Lydgate first appears as the subject of others' gossip, in this case the dinner-party given by Mr Brooke at the outset of his ill-fated political career. The new doctor is rumoured to be 'wonderfully clever' and 'a sort of philanthropist', with new ideas which excite enthusiasm in the host and suspicion in some of his guests (x, 74–5). We are told at some length about his past and about the development of his passion both for science and for women. It is a technique acknowledged in the text to be an artificial convention of fiction, for the narrator self-consciously aims to make him 'better known to any one interested in him than he could possibly be even to those who had seen the most of him since his arrival in Middlemarch', where he is 'known merely as a cluster of signs for his neighbours' false suppositions' (xv, 116). The point is that novels give us privileged access to the inner lives and past experiences of characters who in 'real life' would be much more opaque. It is precisely because they are fictitious constructs of the imagination that they can be made to appear so transparent.

Rosamond, as we have seen, reads Lydgate as if he were a character in a romantic novel. She weaves 'a preconceived romance' around him, 'occupied not exactly with Tertius Lydgate as he was in himself, but with his relation to her'. She reads more into him than less interested observers: 'His looks and words meant more to her than other men's, because she cared more for them' (xvi, 137). His scientific aspirations, which play no part in her dreams of courtship, will later appear to her 'peculiar' and 'morbid', the doubtful activities of a very different man to 'the Lydgate with whom she had been in love' (lxiv, 541). He in turn misreads Rosamond, taken in by her 'eyes of heavenly blue, deep enough to hold the most exquisite meanings an ingenious beholder could put into them' (xii, 91). He too constructs an elaborate erotic dream from a few faint blushes, light glances and gentle touches of the fingertips. And he too becomes disenchanted, looking 'through less and less of interfering illusion at the blank, unreflecting surface her mind presented' to him (lviii, 478). He fails to recognise himself in what she makes of him while she fails to respond to the image he has of himself. Their relationship is built upon shifting signs which are the reflection of their own desire.

Character, then, is presented as a complex business, a matter of illusion and misconstruction. It is neither stable nor unified. Lydgate falls short of his ambitions, acting in opposition to his own highest ideals and taking on a different significance (as a sign), both in his own eyes and in those of others, from what he had intended. The narrator interrupts the story of Lydgate's early life to discuss how,

> in the multitude of middle-aged men who go about their vocations in a daily course determined for them much in the same way as the tie of their cravats, there is always a good number who once meant to shape their own deeds and alter the world a little. The story of their coming to be shapen after the average and fit to be packed by the gross, is hardly ever told even

in their consciousness; for perhaps their ardour in generous unpaid toil cooled as imperceptibly as the ardour of other youthful loves, till one day their earlier self walked like a ghost in its old home and made the new furniture ghastly. (xv, 119)

Lydgate, we are told, 'did not mean to be one of those failures' but loses control over his own meaning, over the development of his own life and the emergence of a self different from the one he had earlier believed in. He did not 'mean' to visit the Vincys as often as he does, and certainly not to marry. He calls himself Rosamond's 'captive, meaning all the while, not to be her captive' (xxvii, 219). But that, of course, is what he becomes. He finally sees himself as a failure precisely because 'he had not done what he meant once to do' (Finale, 679).[3]

The meaning of the self, in other words, cannot be fixed to a stable signified. The 'two selves' that Lydgate discovers within him during his infatuation with Laure: the one that wants to 'rave on the heights' and the other 'persistent self' that 'pauses and awaits' the return to everyday concerns, fail 'to accommodate each other' (xv, 125). There are repeated references throughout the novel to the loss of Lydgate's 'old' or 'former' self, and also to its partial recovery as a result of Dorothea's trust. Her demand that he tell her the whole story of his relations with Bulstrode rekindles the doctor's self-confidence, enabling him to feel that 'he was recovering his old self in the consciousness that he was with one who believed in it' (lxxvi, 624). The restoration of Lydgate's character, however, is necessarily incomplete; he can never recapture the unbroken image of his earlier self (which itself becomes a kind of goal, an imaginary construct at which he can aim).

Nearly all the characters in *Middlemarch* suffer from similar illusions and distortions about themselves and about their neighbours. Fred Vincy, for example, 'fancied that he saw to the bottom of his uncle Featherstone's soul' while actually seeing simply 'the reflex of his own inclinations' (xii, 98). His financial expectations from that quarter alter 'the angle at which most people viewed Fred Vincy in Middlemarch; and in his own consciousness, what uncle Featherstone would do for him in an emergency ... formed always an immeasurable depth of aerial perspective' (xxiii, 193). He loses much of this respect and has thoroughly to alter his own self-image as a result of the disappointment of these hopes. Mary Garth alone laughs at all such illusions, at people 'thinking their own lies opaque while everybody else's were transparent' (xxxiii, 258). Everything in *Middlemarch* turns out to be less transparent than it at first appeared.

In Bulstrode, scorned by Lydgate as an 'absurd mixture of contradictory impressions' (lxvii, 555), the tension between his 'two distinct lives', between the dubious business by which his wealth was won and the pious mastery with which it is spent, becomes psychotic, almost schizophrenic. In the words from *Rasselas* which introduce Chapter 61, 'Inconsistencies ... cannot both be right, but imputed to man they may both be true'. Bulstrode manages for some time to maintain the image of himself as a pious servant of the Lord in spite of his guilty past. But the 'civil war within the soul', of which the epigraph to Chapter 67 speaks, combined with 'a lack of sleep, which was really only a slight exaggeration of an habitual dyspeptic symptom', threatens to disintegrate this self-image, alarming him with the prospect of 'threatening insanity' (lxvii, 556). It is only his wife's understanding and support which rescue him from this fate.

Middlemarch abounds in the misconstruction of character. The most blatant example is probably Dorothea's misreading of Casaubon, on which the narrator comments,

Signs are small measurable things, but interpretations are illimitable, and in girls of sweet, ardent nature, every sign is apt to conjure up wonder, hope, belief, vast as a sky, and coloured by a diffused thimbleful of matter in the shape of knowledge. (iii, 21)

Dorothea's interpretation of the signals emitted by Casaubon is clearly coloured by such a combination of emotion and ignorance. She even admires his letters and speeches of proposal, her 'faith' supplying all that he leaves 'unsaid', just as a 'text, whether of prophet or of poet, expands for whatever we can put into it' (v, 41). Ladislaw recognises the 'romance' she must have made for herself in this marriage, meeting her in Rome just at the time when her attitude is changing from uncritical awe to 'a pitying tenderness fed by the realities of his lot and not by her own dreams', a recognition of his 'equivalent centre of self, whence the lights and shadows must always fall with a certain difference' (xxi, 172–3). Her acknowledgement of his need as a subject who perceives the world differently is the first step in her changing awareness of him as an object separate from herself and beyond her control. The self has become an altogether more fluid concept, a matter of changing relations rather than essential stability.

Dorothea continues, of course, to misread others and to suffer in return from their misconstruction of her. Even her silence becomes to Casaubon's 'suspicious interpretation' a 'suppressed rebellion', provoking his 'construction' of 'imaginary facts' about her and Ladislaw (xlii, 343), who also has a tendency to read emotions into her silences. She in turn misconstrues the motives for Will's visits to Rosamond, failing to recognise herself as the real object of his devotion. She fails to pick up other signs of his interest in her, misinterpreting his embarrassment at the codicil to Casaubon's will, which she sees simply as a rebuttal of a supposed financial interest in marriage. The narrator insists that she is completely unaware of the reasons for her tenderness towards the miniature of Will's grandmother, which she cradles in her hand:

> She did not know then that it was Love who had come to her briefly, as in a dream before awaking, with the hues of morning on his wings – that it was Love to whom she was sobbing her farewell as his image was banished by the blameless rigour of irresistible day. (lv, 447)

'Blameless', an addition at proof stage in the second edition (Clarendon, 535), highlights the point, preserving Dorothea's purity at the expense of her self-knowledge. Only later, we are supposed to believe, does she come to recognise the nature of her interest in Ladislaw.

The extent to which Dorothea does come to recognise and accept her sexual drives, forging a new identity for herself in the process, is one of the major questions of the novel. It is made clear from the beginning that she is struggling to control a strongly sensual nature. Discovering that men find her 'bewitching' on horseback and that she herself 'enjoyed it in a pagan, sensuous way', Dorothea, we are told, 'always looked forward to renouncing' her riding (i, 8). Like Augustine, she plans to be good but not yet. She tries to 'justify her delight' in the colours of her mother's jewellery by reference to the Book of Revelation, 'merging them in her mystic religious joy' (i, 12). She disturbs her uncle by confessing that she sobbed aloud on hearing the great organ at Freiburg, to be told, 'that kind of thing is not healthy, my dear' (vii, 54). Her frequent recourse to sobbing is a clear index of her deeply-felt but unacceptable and therefore inarticulable feelings.

Dorothea's mingling of religious and sexual ecstasy is another characteristic she shares with Saint Theresa, whose sweet but painful joy at the visit of the angel with the fire-tipped spear has so often been seen as a sublimated form of sexuality. Dorothea herself, because of the 'Puritanic conceptions' with which she has been imbued, can make no sense of the 'Renaissance-Correggiosities' with which her uncle's house is filled (ix, 60). But she becomes a provocative work of art in the eyes of Ladislaw and his mentor, Naumann. It has been suggested that the pose she adopts in front of the statue of the reclining Ariadne in the Vatican Museum, her 'breathing, blooming ... form ... clad in Quakerish grey drapery' and her bonnet forming a 'halo' around her braided hair with 'a streak of sunlight' falling across the floor (xix, 155), recalls Bernini's suggestive altarpiece of 'The Ecstasy of St Teresa', an ecstasy in which the religious and sexual elements are hard to separate.[4] Naumann certainly notices in Dorothea a conflict between sensual and spiritual desires, absent in the reclining statue of Ariadne which appears to be much more at ease with its own beauty.

Dorothea, at this stage in the novel, is altogether ill at ease, her disappointment with Rome mixing symbolically with her disappointment in her husband. The ruins of the city and 'the wreck of ambitious ideals, sensuous and spiritual' become associated in her mind with her personal disillusion, 'that ache belonging to a glut of confused ideas which check the flow of emotion'. The scenes of St Peter's continue to haunt her imagination, returning 'in certain states of dull forlornness' (xx, 159). They are indelibly linked with this period of her life in that 'dream-like association of something alien and ill-understood with the deepest secrets of our experience' (xxxiv, 267). Eliot anticipates Freud and even Foucault here in exploring the hazy and irrational area of Dorothea's subconscious, the dream-like links between the apparently superficial levels of her experience and that submerged sexuality which provides her with her deepest sense of identity.

This sexuality, however, cannot be openly acknowledged. It must, at least at this stage in her development, be repressed, passing into painful and confused images. The constant checking of Dorothea's emotion which her marriage requires necessarily reduces her to nervous exhaustion. When she can voice her deepest fears to Lydgate, for example, the 'tears gushed forth, and relieved her stifling oppression' (xxx, 238). Even with her uncle she enjoys 'the relief of pouring forth her feelings, unchecked: an experience once habitual with her, but hardly ever present since her marriage, which had been a perpetual struggle of energy with fear' (xxxix, 319). This 'thwarted energy' emerges in shudders, as she is forced to 'shut her best soul in prison', entombed in her marriage and capable only of 'hidden visits' (xlii, 348–9). She is for ever 'repressing tears', as when Ladislaw visits Lowick church, after which she dwells on the 'weariness' of her life, 'always trying to be what her husband wished' rather than 'what she was' (xlvii–iii, 387–8). Small wonder, then, that Lydgate diagnoses 'self-repression' and recommends more freedom for her to act (l, 403).

There has, of course, been much speculation about Casaubon's supposed impotence, suggested as it is by imagery of dried peas, dried-up streams, stagnant pools, locked drawers, winding stairs and catacombs.[5] Casaubon himself shows little eagerness for insight into these closed areas of experience. 'We must not inquire too curiously into motives,' he announces at Mr Brooke's dinner-table, approving of Dorothea's intention to renounce horse-riding, representing as it does her renunciation of other sensual pleasures: 'We must keep the germinating grain away from the light' (ii, 19). It is a maxim the infertile scholar follows himself, although the more he attempts to hide his jealousy of Dorothea even from himself the more evident it becomes, emerging in such nervous symptoms as the unconscious bird-like movements of his head. Mrs Cadwallader claims that he has no blood, only 'semicolons and parentheses', and that 'he dreams footnotes' (viii, 58). What energy he has is sublimated in scholarship, spent on an unproductive 'Key', a theory about 'the seed of all tradition' which was 'already withered in the birth like an elfin child', showing few signs of nourishing 'the embryos of truth' (xlviii, 391). The sustained imagery of sexuality and fertility underlines what a reader must suppose to be absent in Casaubon.

That Casaubon should spend his honeymoon 'lost among small closets and winding stairs, and in an agitated dimness about the Cabeiri' (xx, 162) – fertility gods of Greece and Asia Minor – is particularly ironic. For his soul is seen to be incapable of 'passionate delight; it went on fluttering in the swampy ground where it was hatched, thinking of its wings and never flying' (xxix, 230). Whether or not he is supposed to be literally impotent (and to discuss the genitalia of fictional characters, as in the case of Daniel Deronda, is a dubious activity[6]), it is quite clear that Casaubon does not satisfy Dorothea's sexual or emotional needs.

Dorothea's own awakening to these needs occupies much of the book. The reader, trained in the conventions of romantic fiction, immediately picks up the way her interest lights upon Ladislaw, especially in that astonishing scene in which his features replace those of the grandmother on whose portrait she lingers:

the colours deepened, the lips and chin seemed to get larger, the hair and eyes seemed to be sending out light, the face was masculine and beamed on her with that full gaze which tells her on whom it falls that she is far too interesting for the slightest movement of her eyelid to pass unnoticed and uninterpreted.

The very thought gives her 'a pleasant glow' and a smile which she guiltily banishes in memory of the young man's harsh words about her husband (xxviii, 226). The point here is that all this takes place in Dorothea's mind. The desiring gaze with which the image of Ladislaw looks at her is simply a reflection of her own wish to be desired by him, a wish that the reader knows has already been fulfilled.

Readers of romantic fiction can also hardly fail to observe the eagerness with which Dorothea fastens on the unfairness of Will's disinheritance, supposedly unaware of the effect this has on her husband. Reading *Middlemarch* is a matter of noticing the 'real' subject of the tense discussions she has with Casaubon about Ladislaw in the middle of the night, and of wondering when she will notice this herself. She continues to press the young man's claims on her wealth, apparently oblivious to the metaphorical extension of her riches to include her body. Casaubon at last is stung into savage reply, forbidding any communication between her and Ladislaw, and she is left 'shrouded in the darkness ... in a tumult of conflicting emotions' (xxxvii, 308). When, the reader must wonder, will the light finally dawn?

It takes the jealousy provoked by twice finding Rosamond alone with Will to awaken Dorothea to her own feelings. On the first occasion she begins to understand her motives at hurrying away from the scene of the duet only in retrospect,

the notes of the man's voice and the accompanying piano, which she had not noted much at the time, returning on her inward sense; and she found herself thinking with some wonder that Will Ladislaw was passing his time with Mrs Lydgate in her husband's absence.

This in turn leads her to reconsider Casaubon's attitude to her familiarity with his handsome young cousin. She feels 'confusedly unhappy, and the image of Will which had been so clear to her before was mysteriously spoiled' (xliii, 355). Learning of the codicil and its specific prohibition of their marriage also provokes 'the stirring of new organs' and 'a sudden strange yearning of heart towards Will Ladislaw' (l, 401–2). After this, even the casual mention of his name by Lydgate makes her cheeks burn, the chapter ending with her dwelling on Ladislaw's likely response to the news.

The repetition both of the farewell scene and of the inter-ruption of Will alone with Rosamond has been recognised as a product of Eliot's conflicting reluctance and determination to drive her characters towards self-knowledge at the expense of innocence.[7] After the first farewell scene, a muted affair in which Ladislaw represses his true feelings while Dorothea remains unaware of hers, she is made to dwell on the past and give vent to a 'passionate grief which she herself wondered at' without understanding it. This is when she is presented as cradling the miniature of Will's grandmother against her cheek and failing to recognise the advent of love (lv, 447).

At the second farewell Dorothea continues to mistake Rosamond as the object of Will's declared love, but the gradual realisation of his true meaning releases her own feelings. Typically, in terms of Foucault's understanding of the relation between repressed passion and Victorian inwardness, it is only in his absence that she can begin to 'think of him unrestrain-edly'. Victorian heroines always indulge their feelings in private and in this case there are additional reasons for Dorothea's feeling that 'some hard, icy pressure had melted, and her consciousness had room to expand' (lxii, 518). A new identity is established through an acceptance of passion, an acceptance which only finds full expression after the second interruption scene when she is shaken not only by sobs but by anger, another previously forbidden feeling.

That Dorothea's passion should be provoked by prohibition (in the form of the codicil) and competition (in the shape of Rosamond) is in keeping with the distortions of desire as des-cribed by Freud, while the access of energy which accompanies her final disparagement of the object of mourning also fits Freudian theory.[8] She has been identified as a victim of what Freud called the Electra complex, which involves an attraction to a father-figure who cannot respond sexually and the choice of a man one can mother and control, which would account for both of her husbands.[9] The claim is not, of course, that Eliot consciously builds her characterisation upon these later psychoanalytic theories but that her detailed mimesis of emotional states lends itself to analysis in terms not available to her.

Ladislaw has certainly disappointed romantic readers by failing to exude the kind of sexual potency that would make him the perfect partner of the sexually-awakened Dorothea. Their hands clasp like those of two children as they look out at the storm, although the accompanying thunder and rain could be read symbolically as a release of dynamic and fertile energy. Ladislaw's long hair could also signify a more laid-back attitude, confirming Middlemarch suspicions of his general laxity; it is certainly a significant moment when Dorothea throws off her widow's cap to set her own hair free. Believing that he has lost Dorothea, Ladislaw can contemplate a life of 'pleasureless yielding' to the temptations provided by Rosamond (lxxix, 640), which appears to confirm that he is not quite as sexless as his denigrators have claimed. This in itself does not make him sexually exciting but it does at least allow this dimension of his character to be considered.

What is remarkable about the characterisation in *Middlemarch* is the combination of this psychological realism, which enables and encourages readers to construct a depth, even a subconscious element in the characters (consider, for example how Rosamond's much-vaunted self-control finally breaks down in uncontrollable hysterical sobbing), with a philosophical scepticism which recognises that all understanding of personality is a construction analogous to the process of 'reading' a character in a novel. The text displays the ideological processes by which we construct identities for ourselves and others, warning of the dangers of misunderstanding, misrepresentation and repression. But it also illustrates the necessity of such construction of character, the need to build believable and, if possible benevolent personalities. The Dorothea with which the novel ends is not simply a liberated woman awakened to her own sexuality, her 'true self', but a carefully constructed moral agent who has trained herself to care for others as well as herself by meditating in her boudoir upon their needs.[10] In the final analysis, of course, she has no 'real' existence but is simply a construct of the reader's imagination.

3

The End of History

One of the ways in which individuals construct a sense of personal identity is by seeing themselves as part of a larger story, in Dorothea's case 'part of the divine power against evil – widening the skirt of light and making the struggle with darkness narrower' (xxxix, 329). In the absence of the faith in God which sustained St Theresa's epic life, as the Prelude explains, it is all too easy for modern St Theresas to find their energy 'dispersed among hindrances, instead of centering in some long-recognisable deed' (Prelude, 4). The narrator struggles in the Finale to find meaning in the decentred 'diffusive' effect of Dorothea's relatively 'unhistoric acts' (Finale, 682). The whole novel, in fact, could be said to describe a variety of attempts to find meaning in history, to construct significant stories within which individuals can locate themselves. *Middlemarch* also moves towards a recognition of a modern form of heroism different from that of St Theresa or Antigone – to cite the models against which Dorothea's life is measured – and from Hercules, Apollo and Theseus, the mythological heroes with whom Lydgate and Ladislaw are compared. The old models of history and of heroism may be at an end but some new sense of a goal, a purpose and a meaning is imperative.

The very idea of history, in the West at least, has been shaped by Christian understanding of a divine origin, a sustaining providence and an apocalyptic end. The Book of Revelation, referred to in the opening chapter when Dorothea speculates on St John's use of gems as spiritual emblems, is 'God's philosophy of history', the key to understanding the mystery of time which the young Marian Evans utilised in her own ecclesiastical chart of 1840 but which she later came to reject. She was particularly scathing about a popular evangelical preacher, Dr Cumming, and his attempts in the 1850s to interpret recent political and ecclesiastical history by reference to the Book of Revelation, identifying Tractarianism as 'the smoke from the bottomless pit' and finding similar roles for other opponents. This, she insisted, was feeble both as biblical interpretation and as history.[1]

Even the Hegelian view of history as the evolving consciousness of the spirit, which fed into Strauss's notion of the Divine Idea, Feuerbach's faith in the self-consciousness of the human race and Comte's Religion of Humanity, the Great Being composed of all worthy men and women, to whose past individuals can turn with pride and to whose future they can contribute, emerges in *Middlemarch* as a necessary fiction, the product of imaginative interpretation. The novel may laugh at those like Fred Vincy who indulge 'that joyous imaginative activity which fashions events according to desire' (xxiii, 194), but it recognises the human need for stories, for a sense of origin and purpose, beginning and end, whether in history or fiction. In calling herself an historian in the manner of Fielding, even if she claims to resist the temptation to disperse her remarks over 'that tempting range of relevancies called the universe' (xv, 116), and in likening herself to Herodotus, 'who also, in telling what had been, thought it well to take a woman's lot for her starting point' (xi, 78), Eliot recognises the extent to which history and fiction overlap. Fiction, in her case, aspires to the status of history and employs its narrative conventions. One of the consequences of this, however, according to Hillis Miller, is an implied recognition that history itself is a form of fiction, a construct of the human imagination.[2] It is characteristic of modernity, as we have seen, to express its knowledge in terms of grand narratives about the progress of the race.

The other dominant feature of liberal humanist history – as

understood by Lyotard – is a belief in the speculative unity of all knowledge, deriving as it does from a common origin. The search for origins, whether of the species, of language or of the true primitive church, which occupied so much Victorian time and energy, emerges in *Middlemarch* as a necessary but ultimately fruitless exercise. Lydgate's dream of discovering 'the primitive tissue', from which all the different tissues investigated by Bichat supposedly originated, comes to nothing (xv, 122). Casaubon's search for the common source of all mythology is similarly futile. He believes that 'all the mythical systems or erratic mythical fragments in the world were corruptions of a tradition originally revealed' (iii, 20). His ignorance of German scholarship, as Ladislaw delights in pointing out, especially of such work as Otfried Muller's *Prolegomena to a Scientific Mythology* of 1825, blinds him to the differences between oriental myths and those of Hebrew origin which he wants to see as the sole source of all myth.

Ladislaw resists the contemporary enthusiasm for exploration into origins, claiming that 'he should prefer not to know the source of the Nile ... that there should be some unknown regions preserved as hunting-grounds for the poetic imagination' (ix, 66). But even he is infected by Naumann with the Nazarenes' desire to recover an original pre-Raphaelite, purely Christian symbolism in art. The orphaned state of so many of the characters exacerbates their uncertainty about their own origins. Neither Dorothea, Ladislaw nor Lydgate has living parents in which to root their sense of identity. Their desperate search for some kind of 'centre' to their lives has been depicted in grim post-structuralist terms:

> Ever so gradually ... the awful truth emerges: that Origins, 'Keys', primitive tissues, sources, historical 'background' – the Ur-texts of an epoch – are arbitrary and fictional rather than real, mere attempts to individually appropriate that metaphysical absence which is every Origin.[3]

Included in this list as 'historical "background"' is Eliot's own project in making *Middlemarch* an historical novel, attempting to recapture the 'original' events of history as it really was.

Eliot's own interest in history is certainly reflected in her *Middlemarch* notebooks. Many of the writers cited in the notebooks are historians, ranging from George Grote on ancient Greece, presumably read in connection with her projected epic poem about Timoleon, to William Lecky's *History of European Morals* (1869) and such specialised works as Rutherford Russell's *History and Heroes of the Art of Medicine* (1861). The concept of heroism looms large in many of the notes she took. In the ancient world, as Grote observed,

> Gods, heroes and men – religion and patriotism – matters divine, heroic and human – were all woven together by the Greeks into one indivisible web, in which the threads of truth and reality, whatever they might originally have been, were neither intended to be, nor were actually, distinguishable. (Notebooks xxxv)

For Grote and Eliot, as positivists, the modern insistence on separating myth from history, fact from fiction, remained imperative. And yet Eliot derived from Strauss's work on the gospels a recognition that myth was not simply inaccurate history but significant narrative, told not simply to record what happened but to inspire religious belief, pointing to a truth beyond history.

Many of the characters in *Middlemarch* strive to gain some insight into history, which they can cling to as truth. Dorothea has a passionate concern for 'the destinies of mankind', yearning after 'some lofty conception of the world' (i, 7–8). She evinces only disdain for 'that toy-box history of the world adapted to young ladies which made the chief part of her education', seeking a more systematic approach to history, 'a binding theory which could bring her own life and doctrine into strict connection with that amazing past' (x, 70). Her puritanical upbringing, 'fed on meagre protestant histories', leaves her totally incapable of understanding Rome, 'the city of visible history'. She lacks the hermeneutic equipment, the imagination and scholarship, to understand what she sees:

> To those who have looked at Rome with the quickening power of a knowledge which breathes a growing soul into all historic

shapes, and traces out the suppressed transitions which unite all
contrasts, Rome may still be the spiritual centre and interpreter
of the world. (xx, 158)

Dorothea, who desperately needs such a centre to her life, fails
to piece together the fragments and cannot connect the seemingly sordid present with the past.

Casaubon the antiquarian cannot supply this lack. He describes himself as living 'too much with the dead ... like the
ghost of an ancient wandering about the world and trying
mentally to reconstruct it as it used to be' (ii, 15). Will Ladislaw
is even less flattering about his 'small taper of learned theory
exploring the tossed ruins of the world' (x, 68). Not only has
Casaubon failed to take account of developments in the study
of mythology which make his own methods obsolete; he has
made no attempt to connect the past with the present: 'such
capacity of thought and feeling as had ever been stimulated in
him by the general life of mankind had long shrunk to a sort of
dried preparation, a lifeless embalmment of knowledge' (xx,
161). The '"Key to all Mythologies"', as Dorothea comes to
realise, comprises 'shattered mummies, and fragments of a
tradition which was itself a mosaic wrought from crushed
ruins' (xlviii, 391). In the words of Sir Thomas Browne,
quotations from whose work occupy much space in the notebooks for *Middlemarch*, Casaubon exemplifies 'a pre-emptory
adhesion unto authority', attempting unsuccessfully to establish belief upon 'the dictates of antiquity' (Notebooks, xxviii).
The epigraph to Chapter 45 of the novel, also taken from
Browne, wittily deconstructs the way satirists look to the past
in order to castigate the present, drawing upon models of satire
which similarly denigrated their own times:

It is the humour of many heads to extol the days of their fore-
fathers, and declaim against the wickedness of times present.
Which notwithstanding they cannot handsomely do, without
the borrowed help and satire of times past; condemning the vices
of their own times, by the expressions of vices in times which
they commend, which cannot but argue the community of vice
in both. (xlv, 361)

So the conservative process continues, perpetually complaining about the present instead of making the necessary connections between past and present.

It is Ladislaw, the product of Romantic attempts to reinterpret the past in the light of the present, filling 'dull blanks with love and knowledge' (xix, 154), who teaches Dorothea to make these connections, enabling her to see the positive side to 'the very miscellaneousness of Rome, which made the mind flexible with constant comparison, and saved you from seeing the world's ages as a set of box-like partitions without vital connexion'. Rome, he tells her, 'had given him quite a new sense of history as a whole: the fragments stimulated his imagination and made him constructive' (xxii, 174). It is the human capacity to construct order from seemingly random pieces of evidence which allows a Romantic such as Ladislaw to construct a grand narrative of human progress, conferring meaning upon history and a sense of purpose to life.

Ladislaw's belief in 'culture', which leads him to abandon a traditional education at an English university for what Casaubon considers 'the anomalous course of studying at Heidelberg' (ix, 66), is another decidedly Romantic ideal. It has been identified with that 'Culture' with a capital 'C' which Lewes attributed to such German Romantics as Goethe and Schiller, who saw it as the vehicle through which Humanity could achieve its full potential.[4] These German literary antecedents, like the comparisons of the young Ladislaw to those rebellious English Romantic poets, Shelley and Byron, find their way into the text of *Middlemarch* in the epigraph to Chapter 81, which ends with Faust resolving 'Zum höchsten Dasein immerfort zu streben' (lxxxi, 646). This clearly refers in its transferred context to Dorothea's constant resolve to strive for the highest level of being, and in Naumann's playful casting of Ladislaw in the role of tragic hero in a play with Schiller's title, *Der Neffe als Onkel*.

The trouble with Schiller's heroes, according to Hegel's *Philosophy of History* (1837), is that their ideals are too high to be realised. They tend therefore not to become 'World-

Historical-Individuals', who arise at the right time and place to accomplish necessary developments in the race, but they nevertheless have a beneficial effect on others.[5] Hegel, Feuerbach and Marx take an increasingly materialistic, decreasingly individualistic view of this process with Eliot herself, in a long review of Lecky's *History of Rationalism* (1865), recognising both elements in the dialectic. Progress, she claimed, is achieved not because

> the multitude ... possess a cultivated Reason, but because they are pressed upon and held up by what we may call an external Reason – the sum of conditions resulting from the laws of material growth, from changes produced by great historical collisions shattering the structures of ages and making new highways for events and ideas, and from the activities of higher minds no longer existing merely as opinions and teaching, but as institutions and organisations with which the interests, the affections, and the habits of the multitude are inextricably interwoven. (Essays, 402)

There is clearly a limit to the influence of single lives in this largely impersonal process. Individuals such as Dorothea, Ladislaw and Lydgate may not achieve world-historical heroic status, but they can affect the institutions and organisations through which change comes about. The heroes and heroines of *Middlemarch* can be identified as such 'higher minds' whose 'unhistoric acts' have an 'incalculably diffusive' effect on the history of their time (Finale, 682). It is a very subdued and relatively self-critical form of the liberal humanist myth of progress.

Lydgate, of course, has his own heroes, pioneers of medicine such as Vesalius, whose lives he tries to emulate: 'A man conscious of enthusiasm for worthy aims is sustained under petty hostilities by the memory of great workers who had to fight their way not without wounds, and who hover in his mind as patron saints, invisibly helping' (xlv, 373). They serve a similar function to Comte's saints of humanity, systematically celebrated in the Positivist Calendar of Great Men, inspiring in individuals a sense of reverence for the past and continuity in the whole of humanity. Lydgate can make sense of his life in these terms as part of the continuing process of scientific discovery, unlikely though he may be to meet with immediate success. When he explains to Rosamond how Vesalius acquired his skeletons and what happened to him in the end, she remains distinctly unimpressed. 'I hope he is not one of your great heroes,' she exclaims, anatomists not having featured in the games of 'guessing historical characters' which is what passed as history at Mrs Lemon's (xlv, 374). Lydgate is altogether unsuccessful in bringing her round to his view of history or heroism.

Ladislaw too has heroic ambitions, which make his actual achievements with Mr Brooke seem not 'as heroic as he would like them to be' (xlvii, 384). Most of the characters in *Middlemarch* have to settle for what Farebrother calls 'a good imitation of heroism' (lxvi, 554). For Fred Vincy it seems a 'heroic project' to save enough money to be able to repay Caleb Garth (lxvi, 550) but it is significant that the book he is suspected of writing, of which Mary Garth is the real author, is called 'Stories of Great Men, taken from Plutarch' and that Plutarch's *Lives*, another of the prominent texts in the notebooks for *Middlemarch*, celebrates the influence of heroic individuals upon history.

There is an ironic dimension, however, to all this discussion of heroism, which is a modern undermining of the myth of the hero so prevalent in the ancient world. If Dorothea is 'a sort of Christian Antigone', as Naumann says (xix, 156), she is not the active rebel against the State but the compassionate heroine of Colonus, comforting the ageing Casaubon. If Lydgate has Herculean ambition to perform strenuous labour in the world, he ends up not so much like the upright hero of Prodicus' fable as like Ovid's Hercules, the victim of a woman, forced into domesticity, having made the wrong choice of ease rather than toil, pleasure before duty. This Hercules spins wool for Omphale before being killed by his wife, who makes him wear a shirt poisoned by the blood of Nessus the centaur. It is a fate anticipated in the novel by Farebrother: 'The choice of Hercules is a pretty fable; but Prodicus makes it easy work for the hero, as if the first resolve were enough. Another story says that he came to hold the distaff, and at last wore the Nessus shirt' (xviii, 154). The limits Rosamond places upon Lydgate prove just as deadly, the doctor himself turning bitterly to Boccaccio (via Keats?) to describe his wife as his basil plant, 'a plant which had flourished wonderfully on a murdered man's brains' (Finale, 680).

Ladislaw too, the sunny brightness of whose hair and disposition have tempted critics to liken him to the sun-god Apollo, sees himself as a Theseus-figure with a mission to rescue his Ariadne, Dorothea, from her monotonous Minotaur. 'You have been brought up in some of those horrible notions that choose the sweetest women to devour – like Minotaurs,' he tells her in Rome. 'And now you will go and be shut up in that stone prison at Lowick: you will be buried alive' (xxii, 181). His indignation with Casaubon becomes more and more outspoken: 'if he chose to grow grey crunching bones in a cavern, he had no business to be luring a girl into his companionship. "It is the most horrible of virgin-sacrifices," said Will' (xxxvii, 296). He resolves to rescue her from Casaubon, although in the end, as has been pointed out, he relies upon her to rescue him from the labyrinth of local gossip. He ends up more akin to Plutarch's Theseus, the first of the Greeks to bring democracy to Athens.[6] The heroism of *Middlemarch* is of a muted, middling kind.

The metaphors of *Middlemarch* have also been seen to point towards a muted, secularised apocalypse, an 'apocalypse emigrating from myth to fiction'.[7] The many references to running as opposed to stagnant water, not least the name of the heroine, contribute to a stream of progress, triumphant in the end over the many hindrances to progress: the labyrinths and winding stairs of Casaubon's mind or the fetters and toils in which Lydgate is yoked. Metaphors of light and fire abound, transforming and transfiguring the everyday world, most famously at the end of Dorothea's long night of disillusioned meditation when she sees through her windows the Bunyanesque figure of 'a man with a bundle on his back and a woman carrying a baby'. Only now the jewels of salvation lie not on the streets of the New Jerusalem but in the lanes of Middlemarch:

> Far off in the bending sky was the pearly light; and she felt the largeness of the world and the manifold wakings of men to labour and endurance. She was a part of that involuntary palpitating life and could neither look out on it from her luxurious shelter as a mere spectator, nor hide her eyes in selfish complaining. (lxxx, 644–5)

History becomes a process in which to engage rather than an object of study, an enlightenment on her part which comes as a revelation, another common metaphor of a novel in which eyes are continually being opened to new vision of new truths. Images of spiritual nourishment, filling and fulfilling, complete this pattern of 'muted apocalypse'.[8] *Middlemarch*, in other words, portrays the end of history not in terms of divine revelation but human progress. Eliot retains a belief in history and even in heroism – demythologised and self-consciously constructed as a sustaining fiction. If post-modernism requires an abandonment of all such grand narratives, *Middlemarch* must be seen as quintessentially modern, a characteristic, though highly sophisticated, product of liberal humanism.

4

The Death of God

Middlemarch is also characteristic of its time in its nostalgia for the lost narrative of Christianity. It has been called 'a novel of religious yearning', even though it abandons any belief in a metaphysical 'religious object'.[1] It explores Dorothea's 'soul-hunger' with a sympathy all the more profound because there seems to be no object adequate to satisfy it. She is forced to cover over the absence of God with a self-consciously subjective religious substitute: a life of devotion to others and a belief in people. The essence of Christianity, Eliot had read in Feuerbach, lay in the kind of altruistic feelings with which Dorothea overflows:

> out of the heart, out of the inward impulse to do good, to live and die for man, out of the divine instinct for benevolence which desires to make all happy, and excludes none, not even the most abandoned and abject, out of the moral duty of benevolence in the highest sense, as having become an inward necessity, *i.e.* a movement of the heart, – out of the human nature, therefore, as it reveals itself through the heart, has sprung what is best, what is true in Christianity – its essence purified from theological dogmas and contradictions.[2]

Middlemarch also embodies the negative side of Feuerbach's thesis, a critique of dogmatic theology as merely the objectification of inner feelings, whether of love or hatred. Providence in particular is portrayed as a projection of self-centredness, a baptising of egoism – most obvious in the figure of Bulstrode, who embodies all that Eliot came to dislike in the evangelicalism of her adolescence.

Middlemarch begins with the question of faith, the search by Dorothea, as by St Theresa, for 'some object' which would give life meaning and 'reconcile self-despair with the rapturous consciousness of life beyond self' (Prelude, 3). Much is made in the opening chapters of the 'intensity of her religious disposition' (iii, 24), her reading of Pascal and of Jeremy Taylor, her sudden impulses towards prayer, her impatience with outward trappings: 'ecclesiastical forms and articles of belief compared with that spiritual religion, that submergence of self with divine perfection' (iii, 21). Her spiritual fervour makes her sister uncomfortable, her uncle alarmed at what he calls her 'excessive religiousness' (iv, 31) and her neighbours indignant at her attempts to be better than the average. Her first action on receiving Casaubon's letter of proposal is to sink to her knees and 'cast herself, with a childlike sense of reclining, in the lap of a divine consciousness which sustained her own' (v, 36). She is also said to seek 'the highest aid possible' to overcome the opposition she expects from Celia on this subject (v, 40). The narrator carefully presents this religious experience as Dorothea sees it, through her subjective eyes, reserving judgement on the objective existence of anything metaphysically 'there' to correspond to the human idea of 'divine perfection' or the 'highest aid' — terms which become ambiguous, open to a literal or a Feuerbachian reading. For Feuerbach it was the human feelings which were 'divine' and worthy of the highest reverence, not their false objectification into dogma.

Dorothea's faith in God is likened throughout to her investment of Casaubon with characteristics supplied by her own enthusiasm. The rector is the first male 'object' on whom 'the radiance of her transfigured girlhood' is seen to fall (v, 37), the language here invoking that scene of transfiguration in the gospels which Strauss interpreted as a rather childish investing of Jesus with an external glory which was simply a reflection of the great esteem in which the disciples held him. Strauss, of course, rejects all such miraculous accretions to the natural historical events: 'compared with the spiritual glory which Jesus created for himself by word and deed, this physical glorification, consisting in the investing of his body with a brilliant light, must appear very insignificant, nay, almost childish'.[5] The process by which Dorothea constructs a perfect Casaubon involves a similar 'loving faith': 'She filled up all blanks with unmanifested perfections, interpreting him as she interpreted the works of Providence, and accounting for seeming discords by her own deafness to the higher harmonies' (ix, 61). The text of his letters, as we have seen, expands as a result of what is once more referred to as her 'faith', which supplies all that his sacred 'text' leaves unsaid: 'what believer sees a disturbing omission or infelicity?' (v, 41). At this stage Dorothea remains an undoubted and undoubting believer both in Casaubon and in that higher object of devotion of which he is the vicar (literally His substitute or representative on earth).

Dorothea gradually succumbs, however, to what Casaubon fears most of all, the spirit of criticism. She begins, like Strauss and his compatriots, to detect in him precisely such omissions, contradictions and distortions as they found in the gospels: 'He had formerly observed with approbation her capacity for worshipping the right object; he now foresaw with sudden terror that this capacity might be replaced by presumption, this worship by the most exasperating of all criticism' (xx, 164–5). The narrator presents Dorothea as still clinging desperately to her faith in her husband and her God, hoping almost for the kind of supernatural scene that Strauss had demythologised. When Naumann compares her husband with Aquinas, we are told, 'nothing would have pleased her more, unless it had been a miraculous voice pronouncing Mr Casaubon the wisest and worthiest among the sons of men. In that case her tottering faith would have become firm again' (xxii, 176). In the absence of such a voice, all the objects of her faith, human and divine, seem to have disappeared. Her 'religious faith' becomes 'a solitary cry, the struggle out of a nightmare in which every object was withering and shrinking away from her' (xxviii, 226). Her 'wifely devotedness' becomes a dismal duty, 'a penitential expiation of unbelieving thoughts' (xlii, 342).

She grows 'altogether unbelieving' in the ' "Key to all Mythologies" ' (xlviii, 391).

The death of Casaubon (and with him, or in him, the death of God, the great patriarch in the sky) comes to Dorothea as a great relief, enabling her to throw off the burden of guilt attached to her unbelief. She continues to trust in the human qualities which Feuerbach saw as the 'true' essence of Christianity, for example, the 'divine voice' of conscience which had made her question what Casaubon called 'providential arrangements' (xxxvii, 307). She continues to see herself as 'part of the divine power against evil' represented by all human goodness. This, she confesses to Ladislaw, is the 'religion' she has been 'finding out ... since I was a little girl', forcing her to abandon prayer of the orthodox Christian kind and to concentrate instead on developing her altruism, her capacity to do what is 'good for others' (xxxix, 321). It is, of course, the religion of humanity, the moral essence of Christianity stripped of all metaphysical claims.

Dorothea, in fact, continues to pray but her prayer becomes the kind of meditation recommended by Comte for the purification of the positivist soul, the strengthening of the altruistic instincts by imaginative exercise. It is a secular form of Loyola's *Spiritual Exercises*. According to Comte, simply to think benevolent thoughts, to dwell lovingly upon others, increases one's capacity to act benevolently, to help others when actual opportunities arise.[4] When Casaubon rejects her arm, offered in sympathy immediately after he has heard from Lydgate of the seriousness of his condition, Dorothea retires to her boudoir for a 'meditative struggle' in which 'the noble habit of the soul reasserts itself': 'It cost her a litany of pictured sorrows and of silent cries that she might be the mercy for those sorrows – but the resolved submission did come' (xlii, 350). She waits patiently for her husband to emerge from the library and once more offers him her hand, a symbol of human solidarity which recurs throughout the novel.

In a later crisis, after interrupting Ladislaw alone with Rosamond for the second time and momentarily losing her faith in him, her earlier meditations on the Lydgates' needs are shown to have strengthened her ability to help them now:

> All the active thought with which she had before been represent-
> ing to herself the trials of Lydgate's lot, and this marriage union
> which, like her own, seemed to have its hidden as well as evident
> troubles – all this vivid sympathetic experience returned to her
> now as a power: it asserted itself as acquired knowledge asserts
> itself and will not let us see as we saw in the day of our ignorance.
> (lxxx, 644)

The fact that she has 'prayed' about them, dwelling upon their difficulties, is seen to enable her to overcome her wounded feelings and act positively towards them. Human providence is thus portrayed as replacing divine providence.

The symbol of Humanity for the Positivists was a Madonna-figure, a woman with a child in her arms. The image of the Sistine Madonna occupied a central place in their places of worship as it did in Eliot's heart. Visiting the original painting in Dresden in 1858 gave her a feeling of 'awe, as if I were in the living presence of some glorious being'. She returned frequently to the gallery for 'quiet worship of the Madonna' (Letters II, 471–2). The many comparisons of Dorothea with the Blessed Virgin Mary assume additional significance in this context. Her simple clothing and plain beauty, for example, are likened on her first introduction to 'those in which the Blessed Virgin appeared to Italian painters' (i, 7). She is said to have the 'pale cheeks and pink eyelids of a *mater dolorosa*' after her long night of meditation (lxxx, 645). Lydgate brings out the implicit significance of these comparisons when he sees in her a sustaining human providence capable of responding to the needs of her neighbours. 'This young creature', he says, 'has a heart large enough for the Virgin Mary', pledging her income 'as if she wanted nothing for herself but a chair to sit in from which she can look down with those clear eyes at the poor mortals who pray to her' (lxxvi, 629). In the absence of a supernatural object of worship, human goodness must take its place.

Dorothea is certainly worshipped by both Lydgate and Ladislaw. 'When one sees a perfect woman', Ladislaw tells

A Reading of the Text

Rosamond, piqued by Dorothea's possible misinterpretation of his presence at the Lydgates', 'one never thinks of her attributes – one is conscious of her presence'. 'You are a devout worshipper,' replies Rosamond with good reason (xliii, 357). Dorothea remains 'enshrined in his soul', making him feel that 'to have within him such a feeling as he had towards Dorothea, was like the inheritance of a fortune' (xlvii, 384). It is the treasury of human goodness to which Eliot turned for her hope in humanity. As the narrator explains, 'we can set a watch over our affections and our constancy as we can over other treasures' (lviii, 473). Such inheritance is presented as the highest credible object of veneration remaining to human beings.

Lydgate too dwells upon the 'voice of deep-souled woman-hood' he hears in Dorothea in the same way as he worships his scientific heroes (lviii, 483). Her faith in him, as the narrator explains in emphatically religious language, inspires him to virtue:

> There are natures in which, if they love us, we are conscious of having a sort of baptism and consecration: they bind us over to rectitude and purity by their pure belief about us; and our sins become that worst kind of sacrilege which tears down the invisible altar of trust. (lxxvii, 631)

The death of God and the abandonment of the visible altars of His service make way, in Eliot's view, for the love of man and the religion of humanity.

Much of *Middlemarch* is given over to a critique of belief in divine providence. The famous pier-glass passage, for example, is an anti-theological parable, passing directly from a discussion of epistemological egoism to the belief in providence evinced by Rosamond Vincy:

> Your pier-glass or extensive surface of polished steel made to be rubbed by a housemaid, will be minutely and multitudinously scratched in all directions; but place now against it a lighted candle as a centre of illumination, and lo! the scratches will seem to arrange themselves in a fine series of concentric circles round that little sun. It is demonstrable that the scratches are going everywhere impartially, and it is only your candle which

67

produces the flattering illusion of a concentric arrangement, its light falling with an exclusive optical selection. These things are a parable. The scratches are events, and the candle is the egoism of any person now absent – of Miss Vincy, for example. Rosamond had a Providence of her own who had kindly made her more charming than other girls, and who seemed to have arranged Fred's illness and Mr Wrench's mistake in order to bring her and Lydgate within effective proximity. (xxvii, 217)

Not that Rosamond is particularly devout; she regards religion as a support for old maids like Miss Morgan. But her family as a whole have an irrepressible optimism that everything will turn out all right.

Fred, for example, nourishes a belief that some 'providential occurrence' is bound to rescue him from his gambling debts: 'What can the fitness of things mean, if not their fitness to a man's expectations? Failing this, absurdity and atheism gape behind him' (xiv, 110). Only hardened pessimists, in his view, can remain 'indisposed to believe that the universal order of things would necessarily be agreeable to an agreeable young gentleman' (xxiii, 190). Unlike Dorothea, Fred spends no time in meditation upon the lives of others: 'this exercise of the imagination on other people's needs is not common with hopeful young gentlemen' (xxiv, 205). He has to be alerted by misfortune and Miss Garth to the necessity of providing for himself, learning the worth and the worship of labour. Caleb Garth lowers his voice in reverence when speaking of work, as if 'saying something deeply religious' (lvi, 458). The 'labour by which the social body is fed and clothed and housed' fills him with such awe that he constructs from it 'a religion without the aid of theology' (xxiv, 207), which for Feuerbach was the only true kind of religion worth having.

Casaubon, of course, is a great believer in providence, which he deems to have 'supplied him with the wife he needed. ... Whether Providence had taken equal care of Miss Brooke in presenting her with Mr Casaubon was an idea which could hardly occur to him' (xxix, 229). The most savage critique of belief in providence in *Middlemarch*, however, comes in its anatomy of the narrow-minded Calvinist evangelicalism of Bulstrode. Just as Feuerbach had seen a contradiction between faith and love, a principle of hatred and fear embodied in such harsh theological doctrines as the hell reserved for unbelievers,[5] and Comte had attacked 'the apotheosis of absolute egoism' in the Christian worship of an omnipotent providence,[6] Marian Evans had lambasted 'the absence of genuine charity' and 'perverted moral judgement' of an evangelical preacher such as Dr Cumming, whose sermons were packed with hatred and self-interest (Essays, 158–9). Bulstrode's beliefs are presented in similar fashion as an amalgam of fear, hatred and self-interest.

Farebrother explains to Lydgate that Bulstrode and the rest of his evangelical set 'do more to make their neighbours uncomfortable than to make them better'. They represent 'a sort of worldly-spiritual cliqueism' which sees 'the rest of mankind as a doomed carcass which is to nourish them for heaven' (xvii, 144). Mrs Bulstrode exemplifies this mixture of 'piety and worldliness', having no difficulty in reconciling 'the nothingness of this life and the desirability of cut glass' (xxvii, 221). At least, however, she is portrayed as caring for her family, urging her husband to pray for their niece Rosamond only to receive the complacent reply, 'Those who are not of this world can do little else to arrest the errors of the obstinately worldly' (xxxvi, 285). Bulstrode so identifies his cause with that of God that he interprets all financial success, however achieved, as evidence of divine favour. But his self-congratulation on the way providence has enabled him to buy Stone Court is quickly undermined by the appearance of Raffles, sardonically referring to his fortuitous tracing of his former employer as 'what you may call a providential thing' (liii, 427). That is precisely what Bulstrode does *not* call this reverse in his good fortune.

The arrival of Raffles overturns all Bulstrode's beliefs. Five minutes earlier, the narrator explains, he had been able to hold the Calvinist doctrine of 'total absence of merit in himself' painlessly as a matter of course:

sin seemed to be a question of doctrine and inward penitence, humiliation an exercise of the closet, the bearing of his deeds a matter of private vision adjusted solely by spiritual relations and conceptions of the divine purposes. (liii, 426–8)

Now these words – sin, penitence, humiliation – take on a more tangible public meaning. He struggles to explain the reappearance of Raffles as part of the 'divine plan', characteristically attempting to clothe 'his most egotistic terrors in doctrinal references to superhuman ends' (liii, 430). But he fails even to convince himself.

That Bulstrode's religion 'remains at the level of the savage', based upon fear, emerges in the way he tries to propitiate his 'threatening Providence' with a modern form of sacrifice, offering to lend a large sum of money to Lydgate (lxi, 506). He is terrified at the prospect of a cholera epidemic, talking to Lydgate of the need to 'besiege the Mercy-seat for our protection', the 'broken metaphor and bad logic' of this phrase filling the doctor with distaste (lxvii, 557). For Bulstrode's God is not one of mercy but of implacable vengeance; all that Calvinism has merely taken his 'selfish passions into discipline and clad them in severe robes' (lxx, 577). The fact that Raffles is so weakened by the ravages of drink and makes his revelations seemingly only to the discreet Caleb Garth encourages the beleaguered banker in his belief 'that Providence had intended his rescue from worse consequences' (lxix, 570). Even after effectively bringing about the man's death by failing to pass on Lydgate's instructions, Bulstrode continues to represent providence as the source of his supposed rescue. By this stage, however, readers have learnt to view this God as self-interest writ large.

What readers are left with in *Middlemarch* and what may account for some of the reported melancholy of their response, is a post-Christian account of the death of God. The passing of so primitive a notion of providence as that maintained by many of the characters could be seen as a matter of celebration. But Eliot finds it difficult, I would argue, to persuade either her readers or herself that the replacement of St Theresa's full-blooded faith with Dorothea's honest doubt and well-meaning morality in a hostile decentred world is really something to celebrate. Hence readers' disagreement about the supposed maturity of her abandonment, or at least modification, of her youthful hopes and aspirations. The death of God leaves a blank which is very hard to fill.

5

The Role of Women

Dorothea's abandonment of 'the false male god'[1] and her enthronement as a human type of the Blessed Virgin Mary have a powerful feminist dimension. 'Love', according to Feuerbach, 'is essentially feminine in nature', a divine quality which women can teach the race.[2] Eliot has often been accused by feminists of suppressing her rage at the constraints imposed by society upon women and of bolstering traditional models of women's nurturing role as wife and mother. There were ambiguities in her attitude to women's suffrage and women's work. But *Middlemarch* includes a witty and incisive attack upon patriarchal attitudes together with an impassioned plea for the broadening of educational opportunities for women to set against this emphasis on the continuing need for 'feminine' values such as love and compassion.

Many of Eliot's essays and letters contain a similar insistence on the distinctive qualities which she believed women had to offer and men too often failed to recognise. A long review of 1854 sees women as having 'something specific to contribute' to the realm of literature in particular (Essays, 53). 'Women became superior in France', Eliot argues, 'by being admitted to a common fund of ideas, to common objects of interest with men; and this must ever be the essential condition at once of true womanly culture and of true social well-being' (Essays, 80). The failure to provide such conditions in Britain is seen to account for the anger of women such as Mary Wollstonecraft, whose warning about the power such ignorance invests in 'vile and foolish women' is reinforced by Eliot in a passage from a review of the following year which anticipates Lydgate's fate:

> Men pay a heavy price for their reluctance to encourage self-help and independent resources in women. The precious meridian years of many a man of genius have to be spent in the toil of routine, that an 'establishment' may be kept up for a woman who can understand none of his secret yearnings, who is fit for nothing but to sit in her drawing-room like a doll—Madonna in her shrine. (Essays, 202 and 204–5)

Eliot's savage satire 'Silly Novels by Lady Novelists' of 1856 accepts that women themselves are sometimes to blame for the contempt with which they are treated, ostentatiously parading their 'culture' instead of relying upon 'sympathy, . . . its subtlest essence' (317). But a number of great women novelists, she argues, have already shown their peculiar strength in this area, their 'precious speciality, lying quite apart from masculine aptitudes and experience' (324). In literature, then, as in life, women had a special emotional contribution to make.

As the controversy over 'The Woman Question' developed through the 1850s, 1860s and 1870s Eliot found herself torn between sympathy for feminist friends such as Bessie Rayner Parkes and Barbara Bodichon, who were campaigning for political, legal and educational reforms, and doubt whether such changes might not interfere with the distinctively 'feminine' qualities she wanted to retain.[3] Even the campaign for higher education for women, which she supported financially, contributing towards the foundation of Girton College in 1869, was in some danger, she felt, of interfering with those 'high and generous emotions' which found their fullest expression in family life (Letters IV, 399 and 401; V, 58). While resenting Spencer and Darwin's increasing emphasis on male dominance through sexual selection (*The Descent of Man* in 1871 presenting the mating of humans and of other animals as a matter of beauty appealing to strength for protection), she accepted that there was an innate biological as well as a conditioned cultural difference of gender. Women not only gave birth to children but were better at nurturing them. The home, as John Wharton had argued in his (1853) study *An Exposition of the Laws Relating to the Women of England*, which Eliot admired, was the 'natural empire of women'. She supported the campaign which resulted in the Married Women's Property Act of 1870 partly because this reinforced women's status within the home (Letters, II, 86).

Middlemarch has been seen to dramatise some of the inequalities of marriage singled out in John Stuart Mill's 1869 study of *The Subjection of Women*, especially the difficulties endured by a man who loses his financial status and finds his wife's lack of sympathy a dead weight upon his highest aspirations. Inequality in marriage, according to Mill, led to a 'counter-tyranny' in women, who often resorted to covert means to achieve their ends. Like Mill, however, Eliot hesitated at the prospect of a complete change in the role of women, especially if it brought a lessening of their moral function: their capacity for gentleness and affection, which was 'the spiritual wealth acquired for mankind' by centuries of mainly female self-sacrificing sympathy (IV, 364 and 467–8).[4]

Such doubts emerge in the text of *Middlemarch*, which begins with an ironic reference to 'the inconvenient indefiniteness with which the Supreme Power has fashioned the natures of women', making it impossible to treat their 'social lot' with 'scientific certitude' (Prelude, 3) and ends with Ben and Letty Garth quarrelling over the question whether 'girls were good for less than boys' (Finale, 678). The narrator records the general regret expressed at the limitations of Dorothea's career:

> Many who knew her thought it a pity that so substantive and rare a creature should have been absorbed into the life of another, and be only known in a certain circle as a wife and mother. But no one stated exactly what else that was in her power she ought rather to have done. (Finale, 680)

The question, like so many other questions in the novel, is left for the reader to decide and Eliot's own indecision is evident in her inserting at proof stage into the final paragraph of the first edition that protest, already quoted, against 'modes of education which make a woman's knowledge another name for motley ignorance', a protest which she then toned down in all subsequent editions (Clarendon, 824).

And yet *Middlemarch* can be read as one long protest against the restrictions imposed by society upon women. The first chapter, whose epigraph includes a lament that 'I can do no good because a woman' (i, 7), explains that women in Middlemarch 'were expected to have weak opinions' (i, 9). Dorothea is portrayed as perpetually battling against limitations in her education, refusing to be satisfied with fashion, embroidery and 'a girlish instruction comparable to the nibblings and judgments of a discursive mouse' and insisting on a wider focus for her energies than village charities and the occasional 'perusal of "Female Scripture Characters"' (iii, 24). While Celia plays airs upon the piano, 'a small kind of tinkling which symbolized the aesthetic part of the young ladies' education' (v, 37), Dorothea wrestles with the problems of the world, defended by the narrator for her 'slight regard for domestic music and feminine fine art' (vii, 53) – the 'feminine' being an addition at proof stage (Clarendon, 64). Small wonder that she fails to fit the boudoir in Lowick Manor, with its faded blue furniture, thin-legged chairs and bookcase of 'polite literature in calf', 'a room where one might fancy the ghost of a tight-laced lady revisiting the scenes of her embroidery' (ix, 61). Dorothea is no such lady; she is a woman, with 'powerful, feminine, maternal hands' which she is portrayed holding up 'in propitiation for her passionate desire to know and to think' (iv, 32).

Dorothea suffers no shortage of advice on what constitutes ladylike behaviour. 'Young ladies don't understand political economy,' announces her uncle when she suggests that experimental agriculture is a more useful project on which to spend money than hunting (ii, 15). A little later he confides to Casaubon, much to Dorothea's chagrin, 'I cannot let young ladies meddle with my documents. Young ladies are too flighty' (ii, 17). 'Woman' for Mr Brooke presents something of 'a problem' before which his mind is apt to feel 'blank'. 'Your sex are not thinkers,' he tells Mrs Cadwallader, refusing to 'argue with a lady on politics .... You don't know Virgil. ... Your sex is capricious, you know' (vi, 44–5). Such 'deep studies' as classics and mathematics, he opines to Casaubon, 'are too taxing for a woman ... there is a lightness about the feminine mind – a touch and go – music, and fine arts, that kind of thing' (vii, 53). He is baffled by Dorothea's failure to understand the principles of painting, which he considers 'just the thing for girls' (ix, 65).

Other male characters in the novel have similarly limited views on women. Sir James Chettam is described as 'ready to endure a great deal of predominance [in a woman], which, after all, a man could always put down when he liked' since his mind had 'the advantage of being masculine' (ii, 18). He expresses similar surprise at Dorothea's failure to fit his preconception of the feminine, for instance when she refuses his gift of a puppy, denouncing the poor creature as domestic, unable to fend for itself, pampered and parasitic. 'Ladies are usually fond of these Maltese dogs,' he explains (iii, 25–6). But then 'ladies' are usually prepared themselves to be pampered and parasitic, confined to the home and unable to earn their own living.

Casaubon, of course, has no doubts about the role of women. 'The great charm of your sex', he tells Dorothea after she has accepted his proposal, 'is its capability of an ardent self-sacrificing affection, and herein we see its fitness to round and complete the existence of our own' (v, 41). He expects her to be 'all that an exquisite young lady can be', with the added advantage of being able to copy Greek characters (vii, 52). He conceals his patriarchal possessiveness when Dorothea lingers over Ladislaw's sketch beneath a thin veil of equally coercive courtesy: 'now we will pass on to the house, lest the young ladies should be tired of standing' (ix, 65). None of these remarks require explicit narrative commentary, although there is one acid sentence about women dictating before marriage so that they may have 'an appetite for submission afterwards' (ix, 59). There can be no doubt, however, about the incisiveness of the feminist critique of patriarchy in the opening chapters of *Middlemarch*.

A Reading of the Text

That Dorothea fails to meet Casaubon's expectations of a wife comes as no surprise, even to the original readers of the novel, who had to wait two months to have their fears confirmed. Her presumption on honeymoon in Rome in questioning the usefulness of his many volumes of notes 'instead of observing his abundant pen-scratches and amplitude of paper with the uncritical awe of an elegant-minded canary-bird' seems to him to fit the role of a spy rather than that of a bride (xx, 164). Return to Lowick brings her 'the stifling oppression of that gentlewoman's world', that 'oppressive liberty' in which her plea for useful employment, 'What shall I do?', receives the exasperating and enervating reply, 'Whatever you please, my dear' (xxviii, 225).

Casaubon soon begins to suspect that his wife is not as 'purely appreciative' and 'unambitious' on her own account as he would have liked (xxix, 229). He has to warn her against interfering in the disposal of his property, which is one of 'the subjects beyond your scope' in which she has been rash enough to offer a judgement (xxxvii, 308). Her uncle continues to warn her against 'getting too learned for a woman' and even Will Ladislaw feels 'a chilling sense of remoteness' lessening his love for her because of 'a certain greatness' on her part, 'nature having intended greatness for men' (xxxix, 318–19). It seems impossible for the men in *Middlemarch* to escape altogether from the patriarchal assumptions of the period.

Dorothea only escapes from Casaubon as a result of his death, which is by no means the first occasion on which Eliot asks providence to perform the violence from which her heroines shrink.[5] A chastened Dorothea now confides to Ladislaw that she understands the constraints imposed by marriage, which 'makes us silent when we long to speak. I used to despise women a little for not shaping their lives more and doing better things' (liv, 445). When she commits herself to a second marriage, itself an act of rebellion against the expectations of Middlemarch, she refuses to remain silent, resisting Will's embrace and holding his head 'away gently that she might go on speaking' (lxxxiii, 663). She is not going to be silenced even by a kiss.

It is Rosamond, rather than Dorothea, who is presented as the saddest victim of patriarchy. She is first introduced as the topic of male chauvinist gossip at Mr Brooke's dinner-party, when a number of representative male Middlemarchers discuss her like a 'prize cow'.[6] In contrast to Dorothea, who is engaged in unladylike 'animated conversation' with Lydgate, Rosamond matches Mr Chichely's idea of a woman, blonde and swan-necked, with 'something of the coquette', laying 'herself out a little more to please us' (x, 73). Lydgate concurs in this view, finding Dorothea a 'fine girl – but a little too earnest' and 'troublesome to talk to'. Rosamond, on the contrary, is 'grace itself ... perfectly lovely and accomplished. That is what a woman ought to be' (x, xi, 76–7).

Rosamond has in fact been fashioned according to such masculine dictates at the kind of establishment criticised by the Schools Inquiry Commission of 1864 for giving too much time to accomplishments at the expense of genuine education.[7] At Mrs Lemon's school, we are told, 'the chief school in the county, ... the teaching included all that was demanded in the accomplished female – even to extras, such as the getting in and out of a carriage' (xi, 78). Rosamond is especially commended for her 'propriety of speech', which means that she has learnt to keep her deepest wishes unspoken, never mentioning to her father her interest in Lydgate and assuring her mother, 'You never hear me speak in an unladylike way' (xi, 80). 'Pray do not go into a rage,' she tells Mary Garth, who is understandably resentful of the Vincys' suspicious attitude towards her, for that too would be unladylike. 'You are always so violent,' complains Rosamond, for Mary to reply, 'And you are always so exasperating' (xii, 94). Rosamond outshines Mary in old Featherstone's eyes by showing no signs of the other 'missy''s fondness for reading; she entertains him instead with a sentimental song which he regards as 'suitable garnish for girls' (xii, 95), the food metaphor reflecting his view of women as objects for male consumption. Rosamond never falls beneath 'her own standard of a perfect lady'. Mrs Plymdale may question 'the use of accomplishments which would be all laid aside as soon as she was married', but that is the whole point of the exercise, illustrating the laws of sexual selection, as two elderly male guests of the Vincys confirm: 'The best girl in the world. He will be a happy fellow who gets her!' (xvi, 137).

This fortune is reserved for Lydgate, the metaphor of possession reinforcing that of consumption. His susceptibility to female charm is presented as one of the doctor's 'spots of commonness', evinced in his unscientific attachment to the French actress Laure, whose attractions include talking little. He is bewildered by the sudden insight he gains into the complex make-up of a woman whose fatal Freudian slip involves killing her husband by accident, a murder which she none the less '*meant* to do' (xv, 126). But by the time he arrives at Middlemarch Lydgate has clearly forgotten what he learnt in Paris. Rosamond strikes him as a model of 'distinctive womanhood', having 'just the kind of intelligence one would desire in a woman – polished, refined, docile' (xvi, 134). The word 'docile', of course, gives the game away. Her pride in him also seems to Lydgate to illustrate 'one of the prettiest attitudes of the feminine mind': a tendency 'to adore a man's pre-eminence without too precise a knowledge of what it consisted in'. She is altogether his ideal:

> For Rosamond never showed any unbecoming knowledge, and was always that combination of correct sentiments, music, dancing, drawing, elegant note-writing, private album for extracted verse, and perfect blond loveliness, which made the irresistible woman for the doomed man of that date. (xxvii, 221)

The point to be stressed is that Rosamond is made that way by the coercive power of male desire, which establishes strict limits to what 'becomes' a woman to know. Lydgate believes that he has found 'perfect womanhood ... instructed to the true womanly limit and not a hair's breadth beyond – docile, therefore, and ready to carry out behests which came from beyond that limit' (xxxvi, 289). Rosamond, he hopes, in an appeal to the natural world reminiscent of Darwin, has all 'the innate submissiveness of the goose' to match his 'gander's strength' (xxxvi, 292–3). These gender stereotypes are made to look foolish when the goose turns out to be less docile and the gander not as strong as he imagines.

It does not take long for Lydgate to awaken from his 'dreamland' and discover that Rosamond is not 'an accomplished mermaid using her comb and looking-glass and singing her song for the relaxation of his adored wisdom alone'. And when he discovers that she is less submissive than he had hoped, his coercion becomes more overt. 'I am the person to judge for you,' he insists when she opposes his request to stop riding in a dangerous phase of her pregnancy; though again it is he who gives in to her request not to be treated as a child, which he does with 'a surly obedience' (lviii, 475–6). He reacts with anger to her attempts to advise him on the way he should conduct his practice: 'he was prepared to be indulgent towards feminine weakness, but not towards feminine dictation' (lxiv, 531). In the marital struggle for survival referred to by the Wife of Bath in the epigraph to Chapter 65 Rosamond is shown to be the better adapted to the conditions. She is more obdurate, tougher and more tenacious. Her voice 'fell and trickled like cold water-drops', capable of eroding the hardest stone (lxiv, 539). Her 'torpedo sting' paralyses him; the need to accommodate her 'held him as with pincers'; 'it was inevitable that in that excusing mood he should think of her as if she were an animal of another and feebler species. Nevertheless she had mastered him' (lxv, 546). Lydgate's Darwinian male confidence in his own strength is finally shattered.

The attack upon patriarchy in *Middlemarch* is mostly subversive. Eliot is unable realistically to offer positive models of emancipation from that period of provincial life. She celebrates what she can of the domestic power wielded by women such as Mrs Garth, looked down at as she is by Middlemarch for her knowledge of grammar: 'no woman who was better off needed that sort of thing' (xxiii, 191). Mrs Garth prides herself on combining theoretical and practical domestic skills, on possessing ' "education" without being a useless doll'. She is also shown seldom if ever to follow her own belief that her sex 'was framed to be entirely subordinate' (xxiv, 200). Caleb's employment of Fred Vincy is the hundredth case, the one question on which he overrules his wife after she has made the previous ninety-nine decisions. Her daughter too wields similar power and influence over Fred.

None of the women characters in the novel emulate their author in escaping altogether from the limitations of Middlemarch. But Eliot's escape is at least adumbrated in the role of the narrator in the text, the wise, sibylline figure who may not be 'so far above and beyond the ordinary classifications of our culture that she transcends gender distinctions'.[8] To know that the novel is a product of a woman who has herself escaped from provincial limits, if only by adopting a masculine pseudonym and writing about them, is to know that these limits are capable of being identified and resisted.

6

The Process of Change

The question of what can be changed and what has to be accepted as inevitable is one of the main issues in *Middlemarch*. Marxist critics have tended to attack the novel as mechanistic and deterministic, even defeatist in the way that it presents Middlemarch as trampling upon and driving away those who attempt to change it.[1] The novel certainly appears less than optimistic about the speed with which radical change can be achieved. But rather than displacing history to the margins of the text – as some critics have maintained (critics who presumably retain a notion of a centre to the text) – or reducing politics to morals,[2] *Middlemarch*, I want to argue, presents a very 'real' picture of the way in which history and politics impinge upon provincial life, balancing the claims of the individual against those of society. Progress is seen to be the result of a gradual, complex and sometimes painful interaction and adaptation both of the individual organism and of the medium in which it moves. The march of this medium, to gloss the title of the novel, is the product of 'middle-class' values such as education and culture. To this extent Eliot can be described as bourgeois, liberal and humanist, belonging to a reformist rather than a revolutionary tradition of social thought.[3] She is by no means blind, however, to the material realities of class, money, work and power as they are shown to operate in pre-Victorian provincial Britain.

'The inevitable march of the human race as a whole', according to Eliot's 1856 review of Riehl's *Natural History of*

German Life, is a gradual historical process (Essays, 290). She shares Riehl's scepticism about 'doctrinaire' politics based upon unrealistic expectations of proletarian and peasant classes. With him she looks to the bourgeoisie to initiate change, to overcome philistine public opinion and to bring 'culture' to the masses. 'The greatest benefit we owe to the artist', she claims, is a contribution to this task by 'the extension of our sympathies' (270). Her own novels are clearly designed to further this process. *Middlemarch* in particular is not only 'A Study of Provincial Life', recording like Riehl the gradual erosion of what a later sociologist, Ferdinand Tönnies, was to label *Gemeinschaft* (local organic communities rooted in family ties and religious traditions) in a society increasingly dominated by *Gesellschaft* (urban, industrialised and devoted to the secular pursuit of self-interest). It is also a plea for the creation of a new sense of fellowship, based upon altruism and the service of others, which attempts to produce its own community of caring and cultured readers capable of bringing about the changes that Middlemarch continues to resist.[4]

'Not all the evils of our condition', explains Felix Holt in his 1868 'Address to Working-Men', 'are such as we can justly blame others for' or remedy by 'changes of institutions'. Learning to 'discern between the evils that energy can remove and the evils that patience must bear' is the mark of maturity and 'good sense' (Essays, 429–30), a phrase echoed in *Middlemarch* in praise of Mrs Garth's 'rare sense which discerns what is unalterable, and submits to it without murmuring' (xxiv, 200). There is a vein of such stoicism running through Eliot's translation of Spinoza's *Ethics*, with its insistence on the need to bear poverty with equanimity rather than rail with envy against the rich.[5] It is echoed, too, in her repeated recommendation of Comte's maxim that our life requires a combination of resignation and activity: resignation to the inevitable and active pursuit of what improvement is possible (Letters II, 127, 134; Life III, 34).

This stoical vein emerges in *Middlemarch* in the pervasive image of maiming or injury, when characters have to resign themselves to facts which cannot be altered. Lydgate, for example, must learn to renounce unrealistic expectations of Rosamond: 'the tender devotedness and docile adoration of the ideal wife must be renounced, and life must be taken up at a lower stage of expectation, as it is by men who have lost their limbs' (lxiv, 533). Ladislaw too must face the possibility of life without Dorothea, a prospect he likens to having 'his limbs ... lopped off and ... making his fresh start on crutches' (lxxxii, 655). But he protests against having his life 'maimed by petty accidents' (lxxxiii, 662) and what seemed impossible, or at least improbable, transpires. The financial pressures of Casaubon's codicil and the prejudices of Middlemarch prove eminently resistible. Determination and action in this case overcome determinism.

It is no accident, as many critics have observed, that the marriage of Ladislaw and Dorothea occurs at the same time as the passing of the First Reform Bill, for the heroine's change of heart parallels that of her country, also turning from an espousal of Tory principles to those of liberal reform in the period of time charted by the novel.[6] The point is that change can and does come about at both a private and a public level but not through utopian fantasies, of which both Dorothea and Ladislaw are for some time guilty. Dorothea dreams of an Owenite colony in which she would 'know every one of the people and be their friend' (lv, 449) while Will also harbours plans for a colony, an 'intended settlement' in the Far West, which provides him with an ostensible reason for returning within reach of Dorothea (lxxxii, 654).

Lydgate's youthful radicalism is also shown to be of an extremely theoretical kind which does not extend to the details of his lifestyle:

> In warming himself at French social theories he had brought away no smell of scorching. We may handle even extreme opinions with impunity while our furniture, our dinner-giving, and preference for armorial bearings in our own case, link us indissolubly with the established order. (xxxvi, 286)

The mature Lydgate, who has modified both his opinions and his life style, may not achieve much in the way of reforming medical practice. Even those 'particular reforms' that he sees as 'quite certainly within his reach', such as prescribing rather than dispensing drugs (xv, 121), meet more resistance than he imagined. But he does at least leave Middlemarch with a fever hospital and better sanitation.

That politics in Eliot's view is the art of compromise emerges in the lengthy discussion between Lydgate and Ladislaw in Chapter 46, whose epigraph quotes the Spanish proverb, 'Since we cannot get what we like, let us like what we can get.' The first paragraph of this chapter specifically links Lydgate's struggles for medical reform with 'the national struggle for another kind of Reform' (xlvi, 375). Will speaks confidently of the imminent overthrow of the Tories and the passing of the Reform Bill under a new government. His enthusiasm for this eventuality is derided by the conservatives in Middlemarch, who discern in his speeches dangerous tendencies smacking of the worst excesses of the French Revolution (xlvi, 378). Lydgate too pours scorn on Ladislaw's projection of this one Bill as a 'universal cure', as if the rottenness of society could be healed by 'a political hocus-pocus'. But Ladislaw replies with the reformist argument that 'your cure must begin somewhere'; for him the main hope lies not merely in the ballot-box (although he has moved beyond Felix Holt's contempt for votes) but in 'the massive sense of wrong in a class' (xlvi, 381). He is prepared to stop his ears to reports of the unreformed activities of Mr Brooke's agents, to the imperfections of Mr Brooke himself – who has failed to make the necessary reforms on his own land – and even to the flaws in the Reform Bill as it stands, for the sake of moving towards the eventual righting of this massive wrong.

Class distinction, of course, pervades Middlemarch. The landed gentry of the neighbourhood, for example, express outrage at the 'miscellaneous invitations' to dinner issued by Mr Brooke, who aims to curry favour with manufacturers, bankers and other professional men in addition to the gentry.

Needless to say, the Middlemarchers sit on the opposite side of the table from the gentry in symbolic enactment of class barriers.[7] The narrator comments, perhaps with a touch of irony but recognising nevertheless a very real change, 'in that part of the country, before reform had done its notable part in developing the political consciousness, there was a clearer distinction of ranks and a dimmer distinction of parties' (x, 72). The incorporation of the middle classes into the electoral system had brought with it a clearer perception of the possibilities of political change, of allegiances based upon political choice rather than birth.

Rosamond, whose ideological construction through language and education has already been discussed, remains keenly aware of class distinctions, suffering agonies over the vestiges of her inn-keeping background which surface in her mother's 'vulgar' language. Rosamond, who can scent 'the faintest aroma of rank' (xvi, 136), fawns upon Lydgate's aristocratic relatives and patronises the poor Garths, whose women were reduced to working for a living:

> Even when Caleb Garth was prosperous, the Vincys were on condescending terms with him and his wife, for there were nice distinctions of rank in Middlemarch; and though old manufacturers could not any more than dukes be connected with none but equals, they were conscious of an inherent social superiority which was defined with great nicety in practice, though hardly expressible theoretically. (xxiii, 191)

Middlemarch displays and dissects with minute accuracy material practices of this kind which comprise class distinction in provincial Britain.

Class, it is clear, is not defined simply by wealth. Mrs Cadwallader's rank depends upon her birth and seems altogether unaffected by the strategies to which she is reduced in order to bolster her meagre financial resources. Local farmers and labourers look up to her as

> a lady of immeasurably high birth, descended, as it were, from unknown earls, dim as the crowd of heroic shades – who pleaded poverty, pared down her prices, and cut jokes in the

most companionable manner, though with a turn of tongue that
let you know who she was. Such a lady gave a neighbourliness to
both rank and religion, and mitigated the bitterness of uncom-
muted tithe. A much more exemplary character with an infusion
of sour dignity would not have furthered their comprehension
of the Thirty-nine Articles and would have been less socially
uniting. (vi, 43)

Mrs Cadwallader, in other words, exemplifies the values of
Gemeinschaft, of which 'neighbourliness' would be a possible
translation, holding the community together in respect for
religious traditions.

Gemeinschaft values, however, are being replaced in Middlemarch by the commercial spirit of *Gesellschaft*, in which
money plays the dominant role. The struggle for power between
the forces of land and money is captured in Mr Featherstone's
outburst against Fred Vincy for being so anxious not to offend
Bulstrode:

And what's he? – he's got no land hereabout that ever I heard tell
of. A speckilating fellow! . . . God A'mighty sticks to the land.
He promises land, and he gives land, and He makes chaps rich
with corn and cattle. But you take the other side. You like
Bulstrode and speckilation better than Featherstone and land.
(xii, 90)

The *Gesellschaft* values which accompany the growing com-
mercialisation of Britain appear in the breakdown of family
ties between the Featherstones and the Waules, motivated as
they are by sheer financial greed. Featherstone's poor relations
feel that he has a duty to remember them in his will, Jonah
arguing that

it was not to be thought but that an own brother 'lying there'
with dropsy in his legs must come to feel that blood was thicker
than water, and if he didn't alter his will, he might have money
by him. (xxxii, 249)

The turn from blood to money in this sentence illustrates the
change of values, the erosion of family ties and neighbourliness
to be replaced by money and market forces.

Even Mr Vincy is seen by Mrs Cadwallader as epitomising

the capitulation to market forces, becoming a kind of weasel in the capitalist struggle for survival, not scrupling to 'suck the life out of the wretched handloom weavers in Tipton and Freshitt. That is how his family look so fair and sleek' (xxxiv, 269). He also tries to undercut his competitors by using the cheapest possible dyes even though they rot the cloth. That Rigg should finally convert the Featherstone property entirely into money is a perfect illustration of the triumph of *Gesellschaft* over *Gemeinschaft* values.

Bulstrode's power, of course, depends on his status as a banker, the source of all money. Before Peel's reform of banking practices in England in 1844 all power resided in individual bankers such as Bulstrode,[8] who 'knew the financial secrets of most traders in the town and could touch the springs of their credit', financial credit being the foundation of that more general credit an individual holds within the community. In Bulstrode's case, this is reinforced by loans and charities which dictate reciprocal obligations, gradually building for the banker a power base which he justifies by its use in God's cause:

> In this way a man gathers a domain in his neighbours' hope and fear as well as gratitude; and power, when once it has got into that subtle region, propagates itself, spreading out of all proportion to its external means. It was a principle with Mr Bulstrode to gain as much power as possible, that he might use it for the glory of God. (xvi, 127)

The point at which the narrative voice transfers to that of Bulstrode can be located precisely at the comma in the final sentence. What is undeniable is that Bulstrode seeks power through money.

Money quite literally makes the world of Middlemarch go around. To be kept ignorant of it, as Rosamond is, for 'she never thought of money except as something necessary which other people would always provide' (xxvii, 221), is to be denied power. Dorothea is forever worrying about its use and abuse and the unevenness of its distribution, threatening to beat the rich 'out of our beautiful houses' for letting the poor live like Lazarus in pigsties outside the park gate (iii, 27). The men, of course, try to put her down by conjuring up the magic term, 'political economy', the mysteries of which are beyond the comprehension of 'young ladies' (ii, 15). 'I have been thinking about money all day', she tells Casaubon, 'especially the prospect of too much', only to be told that these are 'providential arrangements' (xxxvii, 307). She knows precisely what she is giving up in marrying Ladislaw and also the responsibility she is assuming. She is at last entering the hard world of money and must 'learn what everything costs' (lxxxiii, 663).

It is Lydgate's neglect of money, his ignorance of 'the part which the want of money plays in determining the actions of men' (xviii, 147), which leads to his downfall, the expensive habits he has unthinkingly inherited leading him further and further into debt. The priggish young doctor who despised Farebrother for resorting to cards in order to bolster his income finds himself playing billiards for precisely the same purpose. 'I don't see that there's any money-getting without chance', he tells Farebrother, reducing professional success to a form of gambling (lxiii, 528). His 'cynical pretence that all ways of getting money are essentially the same' (lxiv, 541) fails to allow ethical considerations to enter the market-place and leads finally to his accepting from Bulstrode the ill-gotten wealth that Ladislaw indignantly refuses.

It could be seen as a similar limitation in Caleb Garth that he fails to see the importance of money: 'Some men take to drinking', his wife comments, 'and you have taken to working without pay.' Either extreme risks leaving families unprovided for. Garth's inability to manage finance is much less damningly treated than Lydgate's; it merely restricts him to 'the many kinds of work which he could do without handling capital' (xxiv, 206–7). It is hardly to be counted as a fault, rather as an exaggeration of a virtue. For Garth's reverence for work for its own sake, his belief in its value not merely in the market but in terms of its contribution to the community is clearly supported by the narrator. To reduce labour to a commodity to be bought and sold, as Marx argued, is to devalue it.[9]

In many ways *Middlemarch* is a celebration of the secularisation of the idea of vocation, the Victorian version of the Protestant work ethic. Here Eliot departs from Marx, who deplored the division of labour, the separation of intellectual from material activity and the specialisation which he saw as distorting the individual. For Eliot, as for Spencer, increasing specialisation is a sign of progress.[10] *Middlemarch* is about work as a means not only of earning a living but of giving life meaning and purpose. Work is the means by which men (and women when they are allowed) 'shape their own deeds and alter the world a little', as Lydgate hopes to do. The narrator makes no apology for focusing upon his 'moment of vocation':

> We are not afraid of telling over and over again how a man comes to fall in love with a woman, and be wedded to her, or else be fatally parted from her. Is it due to excess of poetry or of stupidity that we are never weary of describing what King James called a woman's 'makdom and her fairnesse,' never weary of listening to the twanging of the old Troubador strings, and are comparatively uninterested in that other kind of 'makdom and fairnesse' which must be wooed with industrious thought and patient renunciation of small desires? (xv, 118–19)

Eliot succumbs to her readers' demand for some element of romance but she insists on portraying a world in which work is of supreme importance.

What links the lives of Lydgate, Ladislaw and Fred Vincy, the three young men whose stories dominate the novel, is the significance attached to their choice of vocation. If Lydgate's 'moment of vocation' occupies most of Chapter 15, Ladislaw's gradual development from dilettante to politician, turning 'culture' to the general good, straddles the length of the novel. Fred Vincy is educated to be a gentleman, defined by an earlier age as a man who could afford not to work.[11] What he learns is the value of work, partly through Mary Garth's refusal to marry 'a man who got into debt, and would not work' (xiv, 115), partly through her father's careful tuition and partly through Farebrother's less happy example. 'I would do anything I could', says the disheartened clergyman, aware of his lack of vocation, 'to hinder a man from the fatal step of choosing the wrong profession' (xl, 332). That women do not even have this option, as we have seen, is a further dimension of the novel's exploration of the importance of work.

Rather than reducing materialist politics to idealist ethics, as Marxist critics have complained, *Middlemarch* presents the medium of society as the tangible arena of man's efforts to improve the world. Lydgate comes to Middlemarch precisely for this purpose: 'What he really cared for was a medium for his work, a vehicle for his ideas' (xviii, 147). This medium, however, as the novel illustrates, is by no means a transparent vehicle; it resists his attempts so vigorously that he is soon deploring the way it sucks him into its petty squabbles. The choice he is forced to make between Tyke and Farebrother for the chaplaincy of the new hospital becomes one small example of the way

> this petty medium of Middlemarch had been too strong for him. How could a man be satisfied with a decision between such alternatives and under such circumstances? No more than a man can be satisfied with his hat, which he has chosen from among such shapes as the resources of the age offer him, wearing it at best with a resignation which is chiefly supported by comparison. (xviii, 153)

There is no escaping the limits which society places upon the choices available to any individual, whether of words, of dress, or of work.

Middlemarch, then, is a novel firmly anchored in the material world which it depicts in such minute detail. It is a novel more Marxist than Marx in its recognition of the power of ideology, the extent to which individuals are the products and to some degree the prisoners of the conditions in which they live. In the words of the penultimate paragraph of the novel, 'there is no creature whose inward being is so strong that it is not greatly determined by what lies outside it' (Finale, 682). The leading characters in *Middlemarch* are involved in a perpetual struggle against those conditions, against the 'world' around them, the 'medium' in which they move. And yet that world, as the narrator from a later age continually remarks, *has* changed. Reforms have been achieved in politics, in medicine, in education and even in the opportunities offered to women. Hence the claim in the final paragraph that the work of individuals such as Dorothea is not futile since it is their action which has made 'things . . . not so ill with you and me as they might have been' (Finale, 682). Like many of the other positive statements in *Middlemarch*, this is a muted claim, a sober and somewhat sad affirmation, the product of a self-critical and sophisticated liberal humanism, no longer full of confidence in the grand narrative of progress but committed to a gradual, difficult and possibly only partial improvement.

Notes

PREFACE

1. Anthony Trollope, *An Autobiography*, edited by F. Page (Oxford: Oxford University Press, 1950), p. 246; Virginia Woolf, 'George Eliot', *Times Literary Supplement*, 20 November 1919, 657–8.
2. Thomas Hardy, *Tess of the d'Urbervilles*, Papermac edition (London and Basingstoke: Macmillan, [1891] 1961), p. 147.
3. James Baldwin Brown, *First Principles of Ecclesiastical Truth* (London: n.p., 1871), quoted in Malcolm J. Woodfield, 'Tragedy and modernity in Sophocles, Shakespeare and Hardy', in *Literature and Theology* 4 (1990), 197.
4. Jean-François Lyotard, *The Postmodern Condition: A report on knowledge*, translated by Geoff Bennington and Brian Massumi (Manchester: Manchester University Press, 1986), pp. xxiii–iv.
5. *ibid.*, p. 33.
6. Suzanne Graver, *George Eliot and Community* (Berkeley: University of California Press, 1984), p. 148.
7. Lyotard, p. 38.
8. *Oxford English Dictionary*, vol. 6 (Oxford: Oxford University Press, [1933] 1961), pp. 154–6.

HISTORICAL AND CULTURAL CONTEXT

1. Suzanne Graver, *George Eliot and Community* (Berkeley: University of California Press, 1984), pp. 10–13 and 28–39.
2. George Levine, *The Realistic Imagination* (Chicago: University of Chicago Press, 1981), p. 253.

3. Gillian Beer, *Darwin's Plots* (London: Routledge & Kegan Paul, 1983), pp. 166–8.
4. W. K. Clifford, *Lectures and Essays*, 2 vols (London: Macmillan, 1901), I, 346.
5. Robert Young, *Untying the Text: A post-structuralist reader* (London: Routledge & Kegan Paul, 1981).
6. John Tyndall, *Essays on the Use and Limit of the Imagination in Science* (London: Longmans, Green and Co., 1870), p. 16.
7. Selma Brody, 'Origins of George Eliot's "pier-glass" image', *English Language Notes* 22 (1984), 55–8; N. N. Feltes, 'George Eliot's "pier-glass": the development of a metaphor', *Modern Philology* 67 (1969), 69–71.
8. Herbert Spencer, *Principles of Psychology*, 2 vols (London: Williams and Norgate, [1855] 1870–2), I, 585, quoted in Sally Shuttleworth, *George Eliot and Nineteenth-Century Science: The make-believe of a beginning* (Cambridge: Cambridge University Press, 1984), p. 158.
9. Thomas Huxley, *Lay Sermons* (London, 1870), p. 137; cp. Ian Adam, 'A Huxley echo in *Middlemarch*', *Notes and Queries* 209 (1964), 227.
10. Wolfgang Iser, *The Implied Reader* (Baltimore and London: Johns Hopkins University Press, 1974), pp. 101–3.
11. Hans Robert Jauss, *Toward an Aesthetic of Reception* (Hemel Hempstead: Harvester Wheatsheaf, 1982), pp. 42–4.
12. Robert Langbaum, *The Poetry of Experience: The dramatic monologue in modern literary tradition* (New York: Norton, [1957] 1963), pp. 206–7 and 226.
13. Catherine Neale, *George Eliot: Middlemarch* (Harmondsworth: Penguin, 1989), pp. 84–5.

CRITICAL RECEPTION OF THE TEXT

1. Harold Bloom (ed.), *George Eliot's 'Middlemarch'* (New York: Chelsea House, 1987), p. 3.
2. Jeanie Thomas, *Reading 'Middlemarch': Reclaiming the middle distance* (Ann Arbor, Mich.: UMI Research Press, 1987), pp. 67–84.
3. J. A. Sutherland, *Victorian Novelists and Publishers* (London: Athlone Press, 1976), p. 192.
4. David Carroll (ed.), *George Eliot: The critical heritage* (London: Routledge & Kegan Paul, 1971), p. 29.

5. *ibid.*, p. 30.
6. Patrick Swinden (ed.), *George Eliot: 'Middlemarch'*, Casebook series (London: Macmillan, 1972), p. 17.
7. John Holmstrom and Laurence Lerner (eds.), *George Eliot and Her Readers* (London: Bodley Head, 1966), pp. 80–3.
8. *ibid.*, pp. 105–6.
9. Carroll (ed.), *op. cit.*, p. 42; Kerry McSweeney, *Middlemarch* (London: Allen & Unwin, 1984), p. 136.
10. Leslie Stephen quoted in Swinden, *op. cit.*, p. 87; Leslie Stephen, *George Eliot* (London: Macmillan, 1902).
11. McSweeney, *op. cit.*, pp. 140–1.
12. F. R. Leavis, *The Great Tradition* (London: Chatto & Windus, [1948] 1962), pp. 61 and 75; Laurence Lerner, 'Dorothea and the Theresa complex', in *The Truth-Tellers* (London: Chatto & Windus, 1967), pp. 249–69.
13. Joan Bennett, *George Eliot: Her mind and her art* (Cambridge: Cambridge University Press, [1948] 1966), pp. 160–78.
14. Swinden, *op. cit.*, p. 61.
15. Barbara Hardy (ed.), *'Middlemarch': Critical approaches to the novel* (London: Athlone, 1967), pp. 3 and 146.
16. W. J. Harvey, 'Introduction' to the Penguin edition of *Middlemarch* (Harmondsworth: Penguin, 1965), pp. 9 and 21.
17. David Daiches, *George Eliot: 'Middlemarch'* (London: Edward Arnold, 1963), p. 69.
18. Graham Martin, *George Eliot: 'Middlemarch'* (Milton Keynes: Open University Press, 1974).
19. Colin MacCabe, *James Joyce and the Revolution of the Word* (London: Macmillan, 1978), pp. 13–17.
20. Roland Barthes, *S/Z*, translated by Richard Miller (London: Jonathan Cape, 1975), pp. 173–4.
21. J. Hillis Miller, 'Optic and semiotic in *Middlemarch*', in Jerome Buckley (ed.), *The Worlds of Victorian Fiction* (Cambridge, Mass.: Harvard University Press, 1975), pp. 125–45.
22. David Lodge, '*Middlemarch* and the idea of the classic realist text', in Arnold Kettle (ed.), *The Nineteenth-Century Novel* (London: Heinemann and Open University Press, 1982), p. 236.

THEORETICAL PERSPECTIVES

1. Stanley Fish, *Is There a Text in this Class?* (Baltimore and London: Johns Hopkins University Press, 1981).

2. Wolfgang Iser, *The Act of Reading* (Baltimore and London: Johns Hopkins University Press, 1978).
3. Carol Snee, 'Period studies and the place of criticism', in Peter Widdowson (ed.), *Re-Reading English* (London: Methuen, 1982), p. 165.
4. Mikhail Bakhtin, *The Dialogic Imagination*, translated by M. H. and C. Emerson, edited by Michael Holquist (Austin, Texas: University of Texas Press, 1981).
5. Ann Jefferson, 'Intertextuality and the poetics of fiction', in Elinor Shaffer (ed.), *Comparative Criticism, A Yearbook*, vol. 2 (Cambridge: Cambridge University Press, 1980), p. 237.
6. F. R. Leavis, *The Great Tradition* (London: Chatto & Windus, [1948] 1962), pp. 65, 75 and 77.
7. Gordon S. Haight, 'George Eliot's eminent failure', in Ian Adam (ed.), *This Particular Web: Essays on 'Middlemarch'* (Toronto: University of Toronto Press, 1975), pp. 22–42 (quoting p. 41).
8. Roland Barthes, *S/Z*, translated by Richard Miller (London: Jonathan Cape, 1975), pp. 67 and 94.
9. Harold Bloom, *The Anxiety of Influence* (New York: Oxford University Press, 1973).
10. Jerome Beaty, *'Middlemarch' from Notebook to Novel: A study of George Eliot's creative method* (Urbana: University of Illinois Press, 1960), pp. 105–8.
11. Elaine Showalter, 'Towards a feminist poetics', in Mary Jacobus (ed.), *Women Writing and Writing About Women* (London: Croom Helm, 1979).
12. Zelda Austen, 'Why feminist critics are angry with George Eliot', *College English* 37 (1976), 549–61.
13. Terry Eagleton, *Criticism and Ideology* (London: Verso, [1976] 1978), p. 121.
14. William Myers, *The Teaching of George Eliot* (Leicester: Leicester University Press, 1984), pp. 103–18.

1. THE PLAY OF VOICES

1. Robert Kiely, 'The limits of dialogue in *Middlemarch*', in Jerome H. Buckley (ed.), *The Worlds of Victorian Fiction* (Cambridge, Mass.: Harvard University Press, 1975), pp. 103–23 (quoting p. 108).
2. Ellen Schauber and Ellen Spolsky, 'Stalking a generative poetics', *New Literary History* 12 (1981), 397–413 (quoting p. 407).

3. U. C. Knoepflmacher, '*Middlemarch*: an avuncular view', *Nineteenth-Century Fiction* 30 (1975), 53–81.
4. Quentin Anderson, 'George Eliot in *Middlemarch*', in *The Penguin Guide to English Literature* vol. 6 (Harmondsworth, 1958), pp. 274–93.
5. Jane S. Smith, 'The reader as part of the fiction in *Middlemarch*', *Texas Studies in Literature and Language* 19 (1977), 188–203 (quoting p. 194); cp. Isobel Armstrong, '*Middlemarch*: a note on George Eliot's "wisdom"', in Barbara Hardy (ed.), *Critical Essays on George Eliot* (London: Routledge & Kegan Paul, 1970), pp. 116–32.
6. David Lodge, '*Middlemarch* and the idea of the classic realist text', in Arnold Kettle (ed.), *The Nineteenth-Century Novel* (London: Heinemann and Open University Press, 1982), p. 226.
7. Rosemary Clark-Beattie, '*Middlemarch*'s dialogic style', *Journal of Narrative Technique* 15 (1985), 199–218.
8. M. P. Ginsburg, 'Pseudonym, epigraphs, and narrative voice: *Middlemarch* and the problem of authorship', *English Literary History* 47 (1980), 542–58 (q. p. 555).
9. Roy Pascal, *The Dual Voice* (Manchester: Manchester University Press, 1977), pp. 78–89.
10. Reva Stump, *Movement and Vision in George Eliot's Novels* (Seattle: University of Washington Press, 1959); Karen B. Mann, *The Language that Makes George Eliot's Fiction* (Baltimore and London: Johns Hopkins University Press, 1983).
11. Peter Jones, *Philosophy and the Novel* (Oxford: Clarendon Press, 1975), p. 49.

2. THE CONSTRUCTION OF CHARACTER

1. Barbara Hardy, *Particularities* (London: Peter Owen, 1982), pp. 12–14.
2. John Kucich, 'Repression and dialectical inwardness in *Middlemarch*', *Mosaic* 18 (1985), 45–63 (q. p. 47); Michel Foucault, *The History of Sexuality*, translated by Robert Hurley, 3 vols (Harmondsworth: Penguin, 1984–8), I, 123.
3. H. S. Kakar, *The Persistent Self: An approach to 'Middlemarch'* (Delhi: Doaba House, 1977), pp. 30–1.
4. Hilary Fraser, 'St Theresa, St Dorothea, and Miss Brooke in *Middlemarch*', *Nineteenth-Century Fiction* 40 (1986), 400–11.
5. Gordon S. Haight, 'Poor Mr Casaubon', in Clyde de L. Ryals,

John Clubbe and Benjamin Franklin Fisher IV (eds.), *Nineteenth-Century Literary Perspectives* (Durham, NC: Duke University Press, 1974), pp. 255–70; Neil Hertz, 'Recognising Casaubon', *Glyph* 6 (1979), 24–41; Barbara Hardy, *The Appropriate Form* (London: Athlone Press, 1964), pp. 105–31; Richard Ellmann, *Golden Codgers* (London: Oxford University Press, 1973), pp. 17–38.

6. K. M. Newton, '*Daniel Deronda* and circumcision', *Essays in Criticism* 31 (1981), 313–27.

7. Laura Emery, *George Eliot's Creative Conflict* (Berkeley: University of California Press, 1976), p. 174.

8. *ibid.*, p. 178.

9. Mildred S. Greene, 'Another look at Dorothea's marriages', *Literature and Psychology* 33 (1987), 30–42 (q. p. 31).

10. T. R. Wright, 'From bumps to morals: the phrenological background to George Eliot's moral framework', *Review of English Studies* 33 (1982), 35–46.

3. THE END OF HISTORY

1. Mary Wilson Carpenter, *George Eliot and the Landscape of Time* (Chapel Hill and London: University of North Carolina Press, 1986), pp. 3–23.

2. J. Hillis Miller, 'Narrative and history', *English Literary History* 41 (1974), 455–73.

3. Jan Gordon, 'Origins, *Middlemarch*, endings: George Eliot's crisis of the antecedent', in Anne Smith (ed.), *George Eliot: Centenary essays and an unpublished fragment* (London: Vision Press, 1980), pp. 124–51 (q. p. 127).

4. Donald D. Stone, *The Romantic Impulse in Victorian Fiction* (Cambridge, Mass.: Harvard University Press, 1980), p. 189.

5. *ibid.*, pp. 188–91.

6. Joseph Wiesenfarth, *George Eliot's Mythmaking* (Heidelberg: Carl Winter Universitatsverlag, 1977), pp. 186–92.

7. Frank Kermode, *Continuities* (London: Routledge & Kegan Paul, 1968), p. 148.

8. Mark Schorer, 'Fiction and the matrix of analogy', *Kenyon Review* 11 (1949), 539–60.

4. THE DEATH OF GOD

1. Mark Schorer, 'Fiction and the matrix of analogy', *Kenyon Review* 11 (1949), 556.
2. Ludwig Feuerbach, *The Essence of Christianity*, translated by George Eliot (New York: Harper and Row, [1854] 1957), p. 60.
3. David Friedrich Strauss, *The Life of Jesus Critically Examined*, translated by George Eliot (London: SPCK, [1846] 1973).
4. T. R. Wright, *The Religion of Humanity* (Cambridge: Cambridge University Press, 1986).
5. Feuerbach, *op. cit.*, pp. 252–5.
6. Auguste Comte, *System of Positive Polity*, translated by J. H. Bridges and others, 4 vols (London: Longmans, Green and Co., 1875–7), III, 348–77.

5. THE ROLE OF WOMEN

1. Sandra M. Gilbert and Susan Gubar, *The Madwoman in the Attic* (New Haven and London: Yale University Press, 1979), p. 506.
2. Ludwig Feuerbach, *The Essence of Christianity*, translated by George Eliot (New York: [1854] 1957), p. 72.
3. Gillian Beer, *George Eliot* (Hemel Hemsptead: Harvester Wheatsheaf, 1986), esp. chapter 6, 'The woman question'.
4. Suzanne Graver, *George Eliot and Community* (Berkeley: University of California Press, 1984), pp. 167–83 and 205–8.
5. *ibid.*, p. 490; cp. Carol Christ, 'Aggression and providential death in George Eliot's fiction', *Novel* 9 (1976), 130–40.
6. Jean E. Kennard, *Victims of Convention* (Hamden, Conn.: Archon Books, 1978), p. 122.
7. Robert A. Colby, *Fiction with a Purpose* (Bloomington and London: Indiana University Press, 1967), pp. 257–8.
8. Gilbert and Gubar, *The Madwoman in the Attic*, p. 523.

6. THE PROCESS OF CHANGE

1. Arnold Kettle, *An Introduction to the English Novel* (London: Hutchinson, 1951), pp. 160–77.

Notes

2. Terry Eagleton, *Criticism and Ideology* (London: Verso, [1976] 1978), pp. 120–1.
3. Daniel Cottom, *Social Figures: George Eliot, social history and literary representation* (Minneapolis: University of Minnesota Press, 1987).
4. Suzanne Graver, *George Eliot and Community* (Berkeley: University of California Press, 1984), pp. 14–39.
5. Benedict de Spinoza, *Ethics,* translated by George Eliot, edited by Thomas Deegan (Salzburg: Institut für Anglistik and Amerikanistik, Universität Salzburg, 1981), pp. 225–6.
6. Jerome Beaty, 'History by indirection: the era of reform in *Middlemarch*', *Victorian Studies* 1 (1957), 173–9; John Purkis, *A Preface to George Eliot* (London: Longman, 1985), pp. 123–5.
7. *ibid.,* p. 136, complete with seating plan.
8. Gillian Beer, 'Circulatory systems: money and gossip in *Middlemarch*', *Cahiers Victoriens et Edouardiens* 26 (1987), 47–62 (q. p. 59). Reprinted in Beer, *Arguing with the Past: Essays in Narrative from Woolf to Sidney* (London: Routledge & Kegan Paul, 1989), pp. 99–116.
9. William Myers, *The Teaching of George Eliot* (Leicester: Leicester University Press, 1984), p. 117.
10. Alan Mintz, *George Eliot and the Novel of Vocation* (Cambridge, Mass.: Harvard University Press, 1978), pp. 16–17.
11. *ibid.,* p. 57.

Select Bibliography

WORKS BY GEORGE ELIOT *(abbreviated GE)*

Novels

All GE's novels are now available in Penguin with the definitive texts being established by the Clarendon Edition, Oxford University Press. I list them here in chronological order with dates of the first edition:

> *Scenes of Clerical Life* (1858)
> *Adam Bede* (1859)
> *The Mill on the Floss* (1860)
> *Silas Marner* (1861)
> *Romola* (1862–3)
> *Felix Holt* (1866)
> *Middlemarch* (1871–2)
> *Daniel Deronda* (1876)

Other Writings

Essays of GE, edited by Thomas Pinney (London: Routledge & Kegan Paul, 1963).

The GE Letters, edited by G. S. Haight, 9 vols (New Haven and London: Yale University Press, 1954 and 1978).

The Legend of Jubal and Other Poems (Edinburgh: William Blackwood & Sons, 1874).

The Spanish Gypsy (Edinburgh: William Blackwood & Sons, 1868), a long epic poem.

The Impressions of Theophrastus Such (Edinburgh: William Blackwood & Sons, 1878), a series of character sketches.

Select Bibliography

Translations

Feuerbach, Ludwig, *The Essence of Christianity* (New York: Harper and Row, [1854] 1957).
Spinoza, Benedict de, *Ethics*, edited by Thomas Deegan (Salzburg: Institut für Anglistik and Amerikanistik, Universität Salzburg, 1981).
Strauss, David Friedrich, *The Life of Jesus Critically Examined*, (London: SPCK, [1846] 1973).

Notebooks

Kitchel, A. T. (ed.), *Quarry for 'Middlemarch'* (Berkeley: University of California Press, 1950), a notebook now at Harvard University Library, the first half of which contains scientific, medical and political details, the second half a series of plans clearly used in the plotting of *Middlemarch*.
Pratt, John Clark, and Neufeldt, Victor A. (eds.), *GE's 'Middlemarch' Notebooks: A transcription* (Berkeley: University of California Press, 1979), which includes a notebook now in the Folger Library and the first part of the Berg Notebook, in the New York Public Library, both of them containing miscellaneous material gathered while working on *Middlemarch*.
Wiesenfarth, Joseph (ed.), *GE: A writer's notebook 1854–1879 and uncollected writings* (Charlottesville: University Press of Virginia, 1981), an edition of GE's Yale Commonplace Book along with some essays not included in Pinney.

SPECIFIC STUDIES OF MIDDLEMARCH
(abbreviated M)

Adam, Ian (ed.), *This Particular Web: Essays on 'M'* (Toronto: University of Toronto Press, 1975), includes contributions from Gillian Beer on myth, David Carroll on 'fact', Gordon Haight on Ladislaw, Barbara Hardy on the passions and U. C. Knoepflmacher on its new 'reality'.
Adams, Harriet Farwell, 'Dorothea and "Miss Brooke" in *M*', *Nineteenth-Century Fiction* 39 (1984), on the development of tragic elements in the process of joining together the originally separate elements of the text.

Select Bibliography

Ashton, Rosemary D., 'The intellectual "medium" of *M*', *Review of English Studies* 30 (1979), 154–68, includes discussion of Comte, Lewes, Feuerbach and Spencer.

Beaty, Jerome, 'History by indirection: the era of reform in *M*', *Victorian Studies* 1 (1957), 173–9, considers the way in which the politics of the period enters the text.

Beaty, Jerome, '*M*' *from Notebook to Novel: A study of GE's creative method* (Urbana: University of Illinois Press, 1960), an attempt to reconstruct the process by which 'Miss Brooke' was incorporated into the original '*M*'.

Bloom, Harold (ed.), *GE's 'M'* (New York: Chelsea House, 1987), reprints some of the best recent essays on *M*.

Clarke-Beattie, Rosemary, '*M*'s dialogic style', *Journal of Narrative Technique* 15 (1985), 199–218, applies Bakhtin's theory of polyphonic voices to an analysis of the text of *M*.

Cockshut, A. O. J., *M* (Oxford: Basil Blackwell, 1966), in Blackwell's Notes in English Literature series, an introduction for students focusing mainly on the characters and their society.

Colby, Robert A., '*M*: Dorothea Brooke and the emancipated woman', in *Fiction with a Purpose* (Bloomington and London: Indiana University Press, 1967), places *M* in the context of fictional and historical struggles for women's liberation.

Coles, Robert, 'Maturity: GE's *M*', in *Irony in the Mind's Life* (New York: University Press of Virginia, 1978), a psychoanalytic approach.

Daiches, David, *GE: 'M'* (London: Edward Arnold, 1963), in Edward Arnold's Studies in English Literature series, still readable, famous for its contention that the Garths provide the moral centre of the novel.

Edwards, Lee R., 'Woman, energy, and *M*', *Massachusetts Review* 13 (1972), 223–38, complains that GE and her heroines are too submissive to patriarchy.

Fraser, Hilary, 'St Theresa, St Dorothea, and Miss Brooke in *M*', *Nineteenth-Century Fiction* 40 (1986), 400–11, explores Dorothea's sublimated sexuality.

Ginsburg, Michael Peled, 'Pseudonym, epigraphs, and narrative voice: *M* and the problem of authorship', *English Literary History* 47 (1980), 542–58, theoretically sophisticated study of the different voices in the text.

Gordon, Jan B., 'Origins, *M*, endings: GE's crisis of the antecedent', in Anne Smith (ed.), *GE: Centenary essays and an unpublished fragment* (London: Vision Press, 1980), pp. 124–51, a deconstructive analysis of the quest for origins and sources in the novel.

Greenberg, Robert A., 'Plexuses and ganglia: scientific allusion in *M*',

Select Bibliography

Nineteenth-Century Fiction 30 (1975), 33–52, explores the scientific discourse in the novel.

Greene, Mildred S., 'Another look at Dorothea's marriages', *Literature and Psychology* 33 (1987), 30–42, a psychoanalytic account.

Handley, Graham, *'M' by GE* (London: Macmillan, 1985), in the Macmillan Master Guides series, for the A Level market, spelling out the political, social and medical background.

Hardy, Barbara, 'Implications and incompleteness: GE's *M*', in *The Inappropriate Form* (London: Athlone Press, 1964), considers the sexuality implied in the novel, including Casaubon's supposed impotence.

Hardy, Barbara (ed.), *'M': Critical approaches to the novel* (London: Athlone Press, 1967), with particularly interesting essays by Mark Schorer on the structure of the novel and W. J. Harvey on its intellectual context and contemporary reception.

Hertz, Neil, 'Recognising Casaubon', *Glyph* 6 (1979), 22–41, a study of the semiotic systems surrounding Casaubon.

Holloway, John, 'Narrative process in *M*', in *Narrative and Structure: Exploratory essays* (Cambridge: Cambridge University Press, 1979), applies structuralist methodology to a consideration of narrative continuity in *M*.

Jones, Peter, 'Imagination and Egoism in *M*', in *Philosophy and the Novel* (Oxford: Clarendon Press, 1975), spelling out the connections between epistemological egoism and moral egoism in the novel.

Kakar, H. S., *The Persistent Self: An approach to 'M'*, (Delhi: Doaba House, 1977), sustained analysis of the accounts of the self provided in *M*.

Kucich, John, 'Repression and dialectical inwardness in *M*', *Mosaic* 18 (1985), 45–63, brings Foucault to bear on Dorothea's self-conflicts.

Lodge, David, '*M* and the idea of a classic realist text', in Arnold Kettle (ed.), *The Nineteenth-Century Novel: Critical essays and documents*, revised edn (London: Heinemann and Open University Press, 1982), pp. 213–38, counters over-simplified post-structuralist attacks on the privileging of the narrator in the text.

Lundberg, Patricia Lorimer, 'GE: Mary Ann Evans's subversive tool in *M*', *Studies in the Novel* 18 (1986), 270–82, presents GE as more subversive than appears on the surface.

McSweeney, Kerry, *M* (London: Allen & Unwin, 1984), theoretically the most up-to-date of all previous introductions to the novel.

Martin, Graham, *GE: 'M'* (Milton Keynes: Open University Press, 1974), a useful handbook designed for Open University students of the novel.

Miller, J. Hillis, 'Narrative and history', *English Literary History* 41 (1974), 455–73, deconstructive reading, bringing out the conflict between GE's belief in objective history and her implicit recognition of its fictiveness.

Miller, J. Hillis, 'Optic and semiotic in *M*, in Jerome Buckley (ed.), *The Worlds of Victorian Fiction* (Cambridge, Mass: Harvard University Press, 1975), pp. 125–45, unpacks the contradiction between the necessarily encoded vision of the characters and the supposedly transparent insight of the narrator.

Neale, Catherine, *GE: M* (Harmondsworth: Penguin, 1989), in Penguin's Critical Studies series, a sensible, rather traditional reading of the novel, quite good on its intellectual context.

Ringler, Ellin, '*M*: a feminist perspective', *Studies in the Novel* 15 (1983), 55–61, a concise survey of different feminist positions in relation to *M*.

Schauber, Ellen and Spallsky, Ellen, 'Stalking a generative poetics', *New Literary History* 12 (1981), 397–413, applies structuralist and pragmatic theories to passages in the opening chapter of *M*.

Smith, Jane S., 'The reader as part of the fiction in *M*', *Texas Studies in Literature and Language* 19 (1977), 188–203, explores the role of the reader in *M*.

Sutherland, J. H., 'Marketing *M*', in *Victorian Novelists and Publishers* (London: Athlone Press, 1976), explores the reasoning and bargaining behind the decision to publish *M* in eight parts.

Swinden, Patrick (ed.), *GE: 'M'* (London: Macmillan, 1972), a selection of earlier criticism in Macmillan's Casebook series.

Thomas, Jeanie, *Reading 'M': Reclaiming the middle distance* (Ann Arbor, Mich.: UMI Research Press, 1987), a lively, personal account of the novel.

GENERAL STUDIES OF GEORGE ELIOT

Ashton, Rosemary D., *GE* (Oxford: Oxford University Press, Past Masters series, 1983), places the novels in the context of GE's intellectual development.

Austen, Zelda, 'Why feminist critics are angry with GE', *College English* 37 (1976), 549–61, summarises feminist complaints about GE.

Bedient, Calvin, *Architects of the Self: GE, D. H. Lawrence and E. M. Forster* (Berkeley: University of California Press, 1972), Nietzschean and Freudian attack on GE's repressive and ascetic morality.

Select Bibliography

Beer, Gillian, *GE* (Hemel Hempstead: Harvester Wheatsheaf, 1986), in Harvester's Key Women Writers series, includes a chapter on '*M* and "the woman question"'.

Bennett, Joan, *GE: Her mind and her art* (Cambridge: Cambridge University Press, [1948] 1966) also tries to link GE's intellectual and creative development.

Carroll, David (ed.), *GE: The critical heritage* (London: Routledge & Kegan Paul, 1971), useful collection of earlier criticism.

Cottom, Daniel, *Social Figures: GE, social history, and literary representation* (Minneapolis: University of Minnesota Press, 1987), ambitious exercise in cultural materialism.

Dentith, Simon, *GE* (Hemel Hempstead: Harvester Wheatsheaf, 1986), in Harvester's New Readings series, also relates the novels to the social history they represent.

Emery, Laura Comer, *GE's Creative Conflict* (Berkeley: University of California Press, 1976), psychoanalytic probing of such elements in the novels as Dorothea's sexual self-discovery.

Ermarth, Elizabeth Deeds, *GE* (Boston: Twayne Publishers, 1985), in Twayne's English Authors series, reconstructs GE's intellectual development, including a section on the often-neglected Spinoza.

Fisher, Philip, *Making Up Society: The novels of GE* (Pittsburgh: University of Pittsburgh Press, 1981), explores GE's portrait of the collective construction of society.

Garrett, Peter K., *The Victorian Multiplot Novel: Studies in dialogical form* (New Haven and London, Yale University Press, 1980), includes a chapter on GE's exploration of 'equivalent centres' of perception.

Gilbert, Sandra M., and Gubar, Susan, *The Madwoman in the Attic: The woman writer and the nineteenth-century literary imagination* (New Haven and London: Yale University Press, 1979), explores the conflicts between rebellion and submission in GE and her heroines.

Graver, Suzanne, *GE and Community: A study in social theory and fictional form* (Berkeley: University of California Press, 1984), sustained analysis of GE's depiction of the evolution of her society.

Haight, Gordon S., *GE: A biography* (Oxford: Oxford University Press, 1968), still the standard biography.

Haight, Gordon S., (ed.), *A Century of GE Criticism* (London: Methuen, 1965), helpful collection of earlier criticism.

Haight, Gordon S. and VanArsdel, Rosemary T. (eds.), *GE: A centenary tribute* (Totowa, N.J.: Barnes & Noble, 1982), includes several essays on *M*.

Hardy, Barbara, *The Novels of GE* (London: Athlone Press, 1959), still a good introduction to GE's work.

Harvey, W. J., *The Art of GE* (London: Chatto & Windus, 1961), classic New Critical treatment of the novels.

Holmstrom, John and Lerner, Laurence (eds.), *GE and Her Readers* (London: Bodley Head, 1966), useful anthology of the contemporary reception of GE's work.

Kennard, Jean E., *Victims of Convention* (Hamden, Conn.: Archon Books, 1978), includes a chapter exploring the sexism implicit in conventions of romantic fiction employed by GE.

Mann, Karen B., *The Language that Makes GE's Fiction* (Baltimore and London: Johns Hopkins University Press, 1983), theoretically sophisticated analysis of GE's language.

Mintz, Alan, *GE and the Novel of Vocation* (Cambridge, Mass.: Harvard University Press, 1978), explores the rise of professional values with particular reference to M.

Myers, William, *The Teaching of GE* (Leicester: Leicester University Press, 1984), subjects GE's beliefs to a radical interrogation at the hands of Freud, Marx and Nietzsche.

Newton, K. M., *GE: Romantic Humanist: A study of the philosophical structure of her novels* (London: Macmillan, 1981), places her in a Romantic epistemological tradition which steps back from Nietzschean nihilism.

Paris, Bernard J., *Experiments in Life: GE's quest for values* (Detroit: Wayne State University Press, 1965), still probably the clearest and fullest account of GE's religious development.

Purkis, John, *A Preface to GE* (London: Longman, 1985), in Longman's Preface Books, pays close attention to historical details in M.

Redinger, Ruby V., *GE: The emergent self* (London: Bodley Head, 1976), ambitious psychobiography, necessarily speculative about GE's early years.

Roberts, Neil, *GE: Her beliefs and her art* (London: Paul Elek, 1975), places GE's work in its contemporary intellectual context.

Showalter, Elaine, 'The greening of sister George', *Nineteenth-Century Fiction* 35 (1980), 292–311, presents GE as a proto-feminist.

Shuttleworth, Sally, *GE and Nineteenth-Century Science: The make-believe of a beginning* (Cambridge: Cambridge University Press, 1984), thorough analysis of the scientific discourse GE shared with people like Lewes, Spencer and Huxley.

Taylor, Ina, *GE: Woman of contradictions* (London: Weidenfeld and Nicolson, 1989), lively if unscholarly biography.

Thale, Jerome, *The Novels of GE* (New York: Columbia University Press, 1959), standard liberal humanist discussion.

Uglow, Jennifer, *GE* (London: Virago, 1987), in Virago's Pioneers series, explores the complexities of GE's writing from a feminist perspective.

Wiesenfarth, Joseph, *GE's Mythmaking* (Heidelberg: Carl Winter Universitätsverlag, 1977), considers the wide range of myths which contribute to GE's work.

Witemeyer, Hugh, *GE and the Visual Arts* (New Haven and London: Yale University Press, 1979), explores (among other pictorial contexts) the art world in which Ladislaw moves.

Index